M000074717

Enneagram

Real-World Scenarios to Help You
Decipher the 9 Personality Types and
Unlock Your Best Self

by Jody and Jeff Sanders

© Copyright 2018 - All rights reserved.

The contents of this book may not be reproduced, duplicated or transmitted without direct written permission from the author.

Under no circumstances will any legal responsibility or blame be held against the publisher for any reparation, damages, or monetary loss due to the information herein, either directly or indirectly.

Legal Notice:

You cannot amend, distribute, sell, use, quote or paraphrase any part or the content within this book without the consent of the author.

Disclaimer Notice:

Please note the information contained within this document is for educational and entertainment purposes only. No warranties of any kind are expressed or implied. Readers acknowledge that the author is not engaging in the rendering of legal, financial, medical or professional advice. Please consult a licensed professional before attempting any techniques outlined in this book.

By reading this document, the reader agrees that under no circumstances are is the author responsible for any losses, direct or indirect, which are incurred as a result of the use of information contained within this document, including, but not limited to, errors, omissions, or inaccuracies.

Table of Contents

Part I:
Getting Started

Introduction

"If you were any type of animal, which would you be?"

If you are anything like us, you hear questions like this all the time. And when you do, you lean back in your chair, stroke your chin, and think "Hm, that's a good question. What type of animal *would* I be?"

The most enthusiastic will give you an answer without skipping a beat. When writing this, we asked our daughter, who answered "llama" without looking up from her coloring book. Later that night, she asked *us* what ice cream flavor we thought she was. My oh my.

Questions like these may seem like trivial small talk, but they are actually tapping into a deep human desire that almost all people, regardless of race, religion, or creed, share: a fascination with gaining a better understanding of who they are. Social media has capitalized on this in recent years and personality tests have become increasingly popular. You can find tests that will match your answers to...well...almost anything.

We have seen tests with titles of: "Which superhero are you?", "What vegetable are you?" And lo and behold, yes, we even found a test that told us what kind of ice cream flavor our little one is. Strawberry shortcake—figures.

Needless to say, tests of this nature are for entertainment value alone, providing little in the way of actual useful information regarding an individual's true personality. However, there are other personality tests of a more professional nature, that base their results on years of research and studies done on a wide range of people. Personality tests of this nature are based on scientific models that seek to explain personality in a systematic way. This means that they seek to identify common patterns that explain important aspects of an individual's personality that predict how an individual will act. All individuals are very complex, so any model of a person's personality reflects only a simplified version of everything that person is. Still, this does not diminish the predictive power of a well-validated model. Consider, for example, if someone asks you to go into the next room and give their daughter a message. In this scenario, you haven't met the person's daughter, but you still go into the other room in an attempt to complete the task. Since you just saw and spoke to the mother, you plan to use this image of the mother as a model to try and identify the daughter. Of course, you don't expect the daugher to be a replica of her mother, but you expect that she may have many overlapping features. You are also aware that your assumption that the daughter resembles her mother may be completely wrong. The daughter may be the spitting image of her father, or, she might not resemble either of her parents at all. Such is the case when we deal with personality types. There will be some people who resemble the qualities of their personality type perfectly, while it may be hard to see the manifestation of the personality type in others. Additionally, everyone is a mixture of many personalities. Just like the daughter may have some physical features that resemble her mother, father, grandparents, great-grandparents, etc, every person has a little bit of each personality type somewhere in them. When we take personality tests, we try to identify our *dominant* personality type, because this type is the one that is most likely to explain the majority of our thoughts and behaviors. Going back to our example, if you had to identify a different person's daughter, would you first request a picture of their mother or great-grandmother? We imagine you'd prefer a picture of the person's mother because the mother is likely a better model of the daughter, even though you would expect to see some of the great-grandmother's features as well.

In psychology, there are often several models that are used to explain the same phenomena. How do we know which ones to use? You may have heard the famous quote from George Box that reads: "All models are wrong, but some are useful." We've already discussed the first half of this quote. No models of personality will perfectly represent all people at all times, but some, like the ones we will discuss momentarily, can give immense amounts of insight into particular aspects of the human mind. One popular model of personality is gauged using the Myers-Briggs Personality Indicator (MBTI), which categorizes people according to the way they perceive the world and make decisions. It distinguishes whether people are introverted or extraverted and considers which functions they use to make decisions and receive information from the world (e.g., through thinking or feeling). The next model to consider is the 5 factor model. It considers five core traits that are associated with innate, biologically-based features. The model uses five traits that predict many behaviors across a range of psychological studies. The five factors themselves are 1) extraversion, 2) neuroticism, 3) openness to experience, 4) agreeableness, and 5) conscientiousness. Another model of personality is the Enneagram, which is a pictorial representation of how nine universal personality types are interconnected and relate to one other. "Ennea" comes from the Greek word meaning "nine" and "gram" refers to the actual image that represents this model of personality. We will spend the rest of this book taking a deep dive into the enneagram— exploring the intricacies of the structure as a whole, as well as dissecting each personality type both theoretically and with concrete practical applications.

Finding Your Type

TEST YOURSELF
www.personalityintel.com/quiz

If you don't already know your personality type, you may be wondering how you can quickly figure it out. Personality tests are a great starting point; however, you'll only get a definitive answer once you learn about each of the individual nine types and feel which one resonates most with who you are at your core. Before you delve into this book, take about 5-10 minutes to complete an online Enneagram assessment at www.personalityintel.com/quiz. We developed this to be a starting point that you can keep in the back of your mind as you take the journey through the rest of this book.

As you embark on this journey, feel free to reach out to us with any questions, comments, or stories you pick up as you progress through the book and towards your growth and self-development. We can be reached at jjsanders@personalityintel.com and we always love hearing directly from you.

With love,

Jody Sanders

Jeff Sanders

Jody and Jeff Sanders
www.personalityintel.com
jjsanders@personalityintel.com

Chapter 1: The Enneagram and the Centers of Intelligence

The name 'Enneagram' is a Greek word meaning nine writings (ennea/nine, gram/a thing written). Each point on the Enneagram represents a distinct personality type – "Type 1," "Type 2," "Type 3," etc. When first learning about the Enneagram, it is easy to get the types and numbers mixed up, so people often refer to types by nicknames that give a snapshot of a trait central to the personality type.

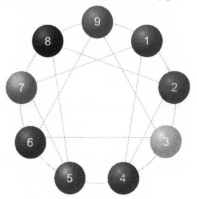

The nine Enneagram types and nicknames are as follows:

- Type 1: the Reformer; the Perfectionist
- Type 2: the Helper
- Type 3: the Achiever; the Performer
- Type 4: the Individualist; the Romantic
- Type 5: the Observer; the Investigator

- Type 6: the Loyalist; the Skeptic
- Type 7: the Enthusiast
- Type 8: the Challenger; the Protector
- Type 9: the Peacemaker

When we first learned about each Enneatype, it never really "clicked" for us until we identified one of our family members or friends that live and breathe that personality type. We could read about abstract concepts having to do with this mysterious idea of a "Three" or a "Seven" all day, but we just had trouble making sense of it until the "Three" and "Seven" had a name and face. We are going to save you some of the hair-pulling we went through and give each personality type a name straight away. Every time we introduce an Enneatype, we will simultaneously introduce you to a character that has that personality type. We'll describe a brief scenario to give a bit of context about how that character acts, thinks, and interacts with others. The scenarios will make the personality types more relatable and give you a glimpse into how each personality experiences the world around them. As we move through each point on the Enneagram you'll meet Susan, (a Two), Alison (a Three), Jennifer (another Three), Markus (a

Four), Peter (a Five), Jane (a Six), Dirk (a Seven), Dana (an Eight), Sophie (a Nine), and Henry (a One).

You might be wondering – why in the world would we start with Two and end with One? If you weren't wondering that, bear with us during this segue.

One of the easiest ways to divide up the nine personality types is into three main centers of intelligence. The three centers are: Heart (Feeling), Head (Thinking), and Gut (Instinctive). In this book, we'll start by investigating the Heart Triad, which consists of Types 2, 3, and 4. We'll then move onto the Head Triad which consists of Types 5, 6, and 7. And finally, we'll discuss the Gut Triad, which consists of Types 8, 9, and 1.

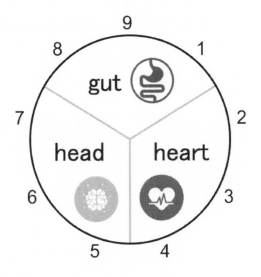

Every person has each of the three centers within them in varying degrees. Head, or thinking, intelligence is probably the easiest for us to conceptualize. Regardless of whether your Enneagram type sits in the Head Triad, you certainly know how to make decisions and become motivated based on processes that occur within your head center, which operates through logic and reason. What separates non-Head types from the head types, is that head types predominately use their Head Center when moving through their world. It is their dominant guiding force in how they act and perceive the world. In contrast, Enneatypes in the gut center will use their head center *sometimes*, but will mostly operate based on processes that occur in the gut center, which is based on visceral, or "gut" instincts.

Each center interacts with and builds on one another, so you can't work on one center without impacting the other two. The more balanced and healthy a person is, the more they will operate equally from each of the three centers. Consider a three-legged stool. Would you be able to sit on the stool if it has one leg that was a bit longer than the others? Sure. But would it be more comfortable if the three legs were perfectly balanced? Definitely.

What if the stool had one leg that was really, really long, and other legs that were pretty much just stubs? It probably wouldn't even be able to stand up on its own! There are people like this too – people who are so dominant in one center of intelligence that it becomes unhealthy. We'll discuss how this can come to be as we journey through each stop on the Enneagram.

In Enneagram speak, we often hear about the word "integration." This is essentially having a perfectly balanced stool. Of course, no one is perfect, so even the most integrated person will likely be a little uneven and prefer to operate from one center of intelligence a little bit more than the others. But even still, the goal should always be to achieve a state where we are balanced in our ability to pull information from our hearts, heads, and guts. To achieve this, a person first needs to become mindful enough to know which center they primarily operate in. Then, they can coordinate all three centers to lead a more balanced and fulfilling life.

The Heart (Feeling) Center – 2/3/4

When we discuss the "heart" we are referring to a person's inter- and intra-personal relationships. Inter-personal relationships simply describe how well you know and connect with other people around you, while intra-personal relationship is how well you know and connect with yourself. When it comes to knowing yourself, your heart should ideally know the truth of who you are as a person and feel secure in your inner sense of self. It lets you know your identity and the reality of who you truly are at your core. It gives you a feeling of significance, value, and glory. When someone says something about you that is genuine and that really resonates with you, your heart opens up and you feel profoundly validated as a person.

When someone has distorted connections with their sense of self and relationships with others, they search for the acknowledgment and approval of others. Everyone starts this way. When we were little, we didn't have the ability of self-reflection. Our identity could only be figured out through others' eyes. When the attention we need is not given, we feel a profound feeling of shame, emptiness, and that something is missing. The heart center types carry this need for validation into adulthood and become highly concerned with crafting a self-image that they believe is worthy of attention.

For members of the heart triad, shame is the dominant emotion that (often unconsciously) leads to unhealthy thought and behavior patterns. Type 2s show their shame externally and create a picture of a good person, Type 3s feel conflicted with their shame and create a picture of accomplishment, while Type 4s disguise their shame and create an image of a unique personality.

The Head (Thinking) Center – 5/6/7

The head center gives us wisdom into the present through the ability to observe, think, and reason. When we can logically assess the world around us along with our position in the world, that serves as the foundation that everything else in our lives can be built on. To some degree, we each need the security of knowledge about the physical world around us. When we lose that sense of presence and feel uncertain about what we can observe and reason with, we lose the ground that is holding, guiding and supporting us – which can make any person fearful and panicky. The head center gives us the ability to minimize uncertainty by observing the current environment, anticipating future events, and making plans on how best to handle those events.

When the head center is too dominant, a person can become paralyzed by a non-stop stream of thoughts and planning to the point that no action is ever taken. On the contrary, if someone does not have adequate access to this center, they may be impulsive and jump into actions without thinking very much at all. As always, the key to success is finding the right balance.

For members of the head triad, fear is the dominant emotion that (often unconsciously) leads to unhealthy thought and behavior patterns. Type 5s disguise their fear by withdrawing into their mind, type 6s avoid internal and external threats because they are conflicted with their fear, while type 7s externalize their fear by keeping their minds busy with activities.

The Gut (Instinctive) Center – 8/9/1

You can think of visceral, or gut, instincts as the feeling you might sometimes get in your body that immediately communicates a piece of information to you. You might feel a sudden disturbance in your stomach that makes you sense that something is off. Or more optimistically, you might experience a deep knowing that you've found the love of your life. Your gut center gives you the ability to instinctively know what is true and not true – a truth that is not necessarily dependent on direct observations and analytical assessments. For members of the gut triad, these types of gut feelings are a major motivating force driving their actions and decisions.

For members of the gut triad, anger is the dominant emotion that (often unconsciously) leads to unhealthy thought and behavior patterns. Type 8s externalize and show their anger, type 9s feel conflicted and separated from their anger, while type 1s disguise and repress their anger.

Diving In

For such a small diagram, the Enneagram houses a ton of information, so don't worry if you already feel like you're in a bit of a whirlwind. Once we start describing more details about arrows, wings, variants, and subtypes – that would just complicate things even further! If you have a general understanding of the three centers, that's plenty for now. We think the best way to really hammer down these concepts is to jump straight into the core personality types in each center. So that's exactly what we'll do now. Once we finish exploring each type, we'll circle back to wings, arrows, and all that other good stuff. Enjoy your journey into the first of three triads we'll investigate: the Heart Triad.

Part II:
The Heart Triad

Chapter 2: The Helper

Enneagram Type 2 is often referred to as the "Helper," or simply the "Two." Twos are those who give themselves to a higher purpose or cause. Often found working in such fields as medicine, social work, and charities, Twos feel a need to help others on a level other personality types will never truly understand. Although the overall nature of Twos is positive and benevolent, there are obstacles and pitfalls that can cause problems in relationships with those with this personality type. This is particularly true when Twos feel that their efforts are unappreciated, which leads them to feel personally unappreciated as a result. Needless to say, this can create significant issues within any relationship, be it personal or professional.

The Two in action

Susan is a principal at the local elementary school. She always keeps an eye out for opportunities to surprise the teachers who work tirelessly alongside her. Dirk and Peter both began teaching one year ago, and Susan is thrilled that she gets to throw them a joint 1-year anniversary party.

As a Two, Susan simply couldn't wait to shower her two employees with appreciation and attention. She excitedly devoted an entire week to getting everything ready. Every day, as soon as the bell rang and the students shuffled out the front doors, Susan made a beeline for her crafting supplies. She made decorations, ordered food, and met with other teachers to delegate the remaining responsibilities. When one teacher canceled last minute and couldn't fulfill her delegated duties, Susan quickly stepped in and got the job done—even though she had a doctor's appointment scheduled during that time. On the day of the party, everything looked perfect.

Dirk, being an Enneagram Type 7, loved the party; he was laughing, joking, and generally being the proverbial "life of the party" itself. Unfortunately, Peter seemed withdrawn and subdued in contrast. He smiled at coworkers occasionally, but Susan couldn't help but notice that he seemed more engaged with his phone than with the actual party. This reaction made

Susan worry that Peter doesn't like his job, or even worse, that he doesn't like Susan.

For the rest of the party, Susan could not stop thinking about all the time and effort she sunk into planning a party for someone who did not even appreciate her hard work. She recounted the nights that she drove home exhausted after a full day of her principal duties followed by party planning. She thought about the doctor's appointment that she missed for Peter's sake. She became more and more frustrated and started to wonder if there were more teachers who didn't appreciate everything she did for them each day.

Since Susan is a Two, she was happy to do something nice for others and in her opinion, she didn't expect much in return – just their respect, love, and appreciation. Since it's in her nature to give others what she thinks they want (i.e., a party), she expects that others will naturally give her what she wants (i.e., appreciation). Unfortunately for Susan, Dirk and Peter did not understand that Susan was looking for their validation. Even still, Dirk managed to give Susan what she needed, while Peter could not. This is only because Dirk and

Peter differ in how they react to social situations and had no bearing on how they feel about Susan. Dirk loves being the center of attention in all things. However, as an Enneagram Type 5, Peter is far from comfortable with any form of attention, especially in a social setting. Therefore, while Peter was happy to know that Susan appreciates his work, he would have preferred a card or a private display of appreciation. Furthermore, as a Five, he also has a hard time expressing his feelings, meaning that even if he was having fun at the party, it would be near impossible to tell.

Unfortunately for Susan, people do not always recognize what others need and even when they do, they don't always prioritize fulfilling those needs. Susan should have placed more value in taking care of herself. If she showed herself more love and appreciation, she might not look for that love and appreciation from others.

Personality profile of the Two

Twos are usually extroverted by nature, which stems from attempts to make themselves available and offer help, even to people they do not know. Unlike other extroverted types, however, Twos are primarily motivated by deep levels of love and devotion. Thus, they are not extroverted in an egotistical sense, rather they are outgoing in order to learn exactly how they can be of service to you.

Twos are also very focused on the things that will help to improve a person's life or state of mind. This is especially true in the case of birthdays, anniversaries, or any other milestone event that deserves recognition. Not only will a Two remember each and every birthday and event, but they will also know the perfect way to celebrate. Whether it's hosting a theme party, choosing the right restaurant or movie to go to, or finding that perfect gift that shows love and appreciation, Twos know how to provide the perfect touch.

Twos are part of the heart center, which consists of the Enneatypes strongly motivated by emotional connection. Twos connect with others by directing love outwards and helping those around them. They often aren't the type to get a job done and rest afterwards. Instead, they enjoy constantly finding ways to be of assistance. When one job is done, they seek out the next job, rarely taking a breath in-between. The simple truth of the matter is that helping others gives the Two purpose, as well as the energy to fulfill that purpose. When a Two cannot find someone to help or a cause to serve, they might even be left feeling as though their life has become stagnant and meaningless.

When we met Susan, we learned how an outward focus could become detrimental to one's own being. Twos often neglect taking proper care of themselves and place all of their energy into making sure everyone *else* is taken care of. Unfortunately, this can result in Twos becoming overworked, overstretched, and generally burned out. An overworked person cannot perform at their physical or emotional best. Circumstances become even worse when being overworked is coupled with a lack of appreciation. Unfortunately, Twos often face the challenge of feeling unappreciated, even though others are not neglecting them for any sinister reason. The fact is that Twos seem as if they were born to help, thus their actions seem nearly effortless. As a result, many people in a Twos life will take their actions for granted.

A common misconception of the Two is that they don't necessarily help others for the pure sake of helping, but rather that they help to display a righteous image to the world and to get love and adoration back from people in return. This idea is only partially true. As part of the heart center, Twos strongly value an image of themselves that they consider to be the core (at the "heart") of their identity. For the Two, this is an image of being unselfish. Since Twos are so focused on projecting their energy outward, they often forget to look inward to reflect on who they are and assess if their values match the person they wish to be. The Two wishes to be a loving, helpful, unselfish person – but they cannot validate that they are loving, helpful, and unselfish by themselves because they do not like to focus on themselves. That is why a Two sometimes feels that they must build up their ideal of the perfect image – so that others can notice what they have achieved and validate that they are indeed loving and helpful. If a Two is displaying an image of being helpful, it is likely because they have a need for recognition that they cannot satisfy by themselves. Twos may not even recognize their need for love, appreciation, and recognition because of their preoccupation with helping. If their needs are not met, a sense of frustration and hostility can start to build up, and eventually the Two may have an outburst that is completely unexpected.

Just like Susan should have focused on her own physical needs by not missing her doctor's appointment, she would also benefit from learning how to self-reflect and identify her own wants, needs, and desires. By self-reflecting, she can also start to develop a sense of self-worth that is detached from whether people are praising her for being so generous and helpful. A Two can only be of true value when they take proper care of themselves. Thus, they need to learn to take time out for themselves to recharge their physical and mental batteries even when the job is still unfinished.

If you recognize a Two in your life, it is critical that you frequently show them true and genuine appreciation, as they need recognition in order to feel validated. They may not request your praise and may even seem to downplay their acts of kindness, but your sincere appreciation will validate their alignment with the ideals that they constantly strive to achieve.

Note that in the above paragraph, we mention the importance of expressing your *true* and *genuine* appreciation to the Twos in your life. What if you just aren't truly and genuinely appreciative? Does that make you a bad person? No, Twos come in many different flavors and not all Twos are on a path to sainthood. There are Twos who give love to get love – even when their help is unwanted. These unhealthy Twos can appear overbearing and people-pleasing. On the other end of the spectrum, there are people like Mother Theresa, who is famously a Two. These healthy Twos love unconditionally, are in tune with themselves, and can recognize and attend to their own needs and desires.

If you are a Two, you have the gift to show endless amounts of love to everyone around you. Your gift can be used to bring smiles to peoples' faces, to alleviate suffering, and to change the world. But just as other's have needs that you can help fulfill, YOU have needs that you can help fulfill. Don't forget to save a little bit of your special gift for yourself.

Chapter 3: The Achiever and Performer

Enneagram Type 3 is often referred to as the "Achiever," the "Performer," or simply the "Three." People in this category are the ones commonly dubbed the 'go-getters.' Threes will devote their time and energy to becoming the best, never settling for anything less. Their goal isn't perfection as is the case with other personality types, rather the Three's goal is achieving status. Thus, they do not necessarily pursue success for the sake of the project, rather they seek it for the personal validation it brings.

The Three in action

Alison, Jennifer, and Henry are participating in a company-wide contest to develop a new marketing plan for Café Fresh, a chain of coffee shops. The team is eager and excited about the project and they immediately grab a conference room to start mapping out their strategy. At 5pm, Jennifer packs up to leave for the day, mentioning that she needs to head over to her son's award ceremony. Alison and Henry, in contrast, continue to work until 9pm. The next morning, Alison and Henry arrive back at work with bagels and coffee they grabbed from Café Fresh. Jennifer comes in with a homemade fruit and vegetable smoothie. This is no surprise to Alison and Henry, who both know that Jennifer manages to make and eat breakfast with her family every single morning – even during important projects like the one they are all working on now. There's a reason she has the nickname "Supermom." Lucky for them, Jennifer also doubled the casserole recipe she made last night so that Alison and Henry can have a home-cooked dinner if they decide to work late.

The team is at it again until 5pm, when Jennifer gets up and begins packing her belongings. The three take the opportunity to reflect on how much progress they've made that day. They all seem satisfied with the strategy they are developing and are excited to finish the plan and present it to the company at the end of the week. Jennifer wishes she could stay, but needs to go volunteer at her daughter's school in just 25 minutes. Alison and Henry don't mind –

especially because they are about to dig into the casserole she made just for them.

On the day of the presentation, the team feels confident in their work and excited to present it to the company. Alison walks confidently to the microphone in her best suit and heels and opens the presentation with a riveting introduction that she rehearsed tirelessly the night before. Jennifer takes the next section because it is her personal passion. She gets the audience excited by explaining why THIS is the most important part of the presentation and then presents the marketing plan flawlessly. Henry ends the presentation strong by clarifying any areas he thinks might still be ambiguous, and effortlessly answers each question posed by the audience. At the end, the company is impressed, and the three are offered a plaque for their exceptional work. Alison jumps up, thrilled, to collect the plaque. When the meeting disperses, Alison excitedly hangs up the plaque and spends the rest of the day chatting with coworkers describing the new marketing plan.

Jennifer grows frustrated as the day progresses and confides in Henry. She thinks there should have been a conversation about where the plaque would be kept. She also doesn't like that Alison casually forgets to give appropriate credit when discussing the marketing plan with others. Henry consoles Jennifer, but personally thinks Alison's actions aren't harming anyone. He doesn't have an opinion on where the plaque is held, but offers to speak to Alison if necessary.

Why does Alison's behavior rub Jennifer the wrong way, while Henry seems unaffected? The conflict here arises because both Alison and Jennifer are Threes. They both seek to achieve their ideal image of success and hope to get validation from the people around them. For Alison, success is equivalent to accolades at work, so she works around the clock to make sure she is on top of her game in the office. Jennifer also values work accomplishments, but her definition of success is centered around her self-image of being a "Supermom." Even still, she believed she contributed a great deal to the marketing strategy and presentation and should have been able to showcase the plaque in her own office.

Henry, on the other hand, is a Type 1 on the Enneagram. Like Alison, he is hyper-focused on work and was happy to put in long days to make sure the new marketing plan was perfect. When it came to external accolades, however, he could take it or leave it. The internal sense of satisfaction was enough for him.

Personality profile of the Three

Threes are usually the ones eager to win and constantly striving to be the best in whatever area they find themselves in. For them, a silver medal isn't 'second winner' – it's 'first loser.' It's not enough to be successful, attractive, or talented— they want to be the most successful, the most attractive, and the most talented. Threes, though, not only want to be the best – they also want people to recognize what they have accomplished and acknowledge that they are, indeed, the best. For this reason, Threes are usually full of energy, charismatic, and extroverted in their demeanors. Needless to say, the times they fail to achieve first place are times of failure in their eyes. It's no surprise that many Threes pursue their success in competitive areas such as sports, politics, and business. However, a Three can also aim to be the best within industries that are not inherently competitive.

We saw this when we met Jennifer. While it was important to Jennifer that she perform well at work, it was more important to her that she was the best "Supermom" in the room at all times.

As part of the heart center, or the Enneatypes most concerned with their identity (the values at their "core" or "heart"), Threes do not necessarily aim to achieve perfection in every area they encounter. Instead, they aim to appear successful to others. A Three's identity, then, is not necessarily about who they *are* as a person, but is instead, about what they *do*. Thus, a Three will pursue success in the areas that they believe will give them the most accolades. They take on the idea of success as defined by the people around them. If, from a young age, one Three is taught that the best achievements come in the form of dominating in sports and having fans stop you in the street – that person will likely pursue sports and rise to the top. If another Three is taught that superior intellect is the pinnacle of success, that person may pursue several degrees. If another Three is taught that endless amounts of money will bring the most recognition – that person may rise in the ranks of business. If yet another Three is taught that beauty is the most valued attribute – they may pursue compliments by ensuring they are always the most beautiful and well-dressed person in the room. Since a Three's definition of success is not internally generated, it can also change easily when they notice potential new areas where they can receive accolades. For example, if Jennifer eventually starts to perceive that people value work achievements more than her achievements as a Supermom, we may start to see a shift in the way she allocates her energy. Do you think it's possible for Jennifer to become so obsessed with chasing work success that she neglects her children altogether? This is unlikely. Most Threes are not praise-hungry machines with no other facets to their personalities. It is important to note that a person's dominant type is never the only aspect of their personality – it is simply the best model to explain a significant amount of the way they relate to the world.

The heart center is often called the "feeling center" because Enneatypes in this triad are motivated by emotional connection. This can cause a bit of confusion when discussing Threes, as they are the heart types *least* likely to have access to their feelings. Though Threes may be motivated by feelings of inadequacy and fear of failure, they often do not have the time to experience these feelings, as they push them aside to focus on the actions they can take to eliminate the areas of inadequacy that are concerning to them. Why, then, are Threes considered part of the feeling triad? Threes get their energy from their emotional connections with *other people*. The gold medal itself isn't the goal, rather it's the adoration of others that the Three truly craves. When success is finally achieved, it will feel empty if it is not followed with adoration to provide the Three with a sense of validation. Threes are driven by the need to ensure they are eliciting positive feelings from *others* and this is what drives them to perform. When we say "positive feelings," though, we use the word "positive" loosely. If you know an unhealthy Three, their competitiveness may be dominating, condescending, and generally unpleasant. An unhealthy Three will tear others down to lift themselves up. They will flaunt their successes and speak of them at length to anyone who will listen. When they run out of accomplishments to discuss, they will make up several more. If a Three relates to you in this way, you may not experience any "positive feelings," per se. However, the Three's *motivation* is to elicit awe and admiration from you – even though they may not succeed in doing so.

A Three's primary motivation is to inspire awe and admiration from the people around them. They can achieve this through 1) taking action and becoming great in one or more areas, 2) telling people they are great in one or more areas, or 3) some combination of the two. We already hinted at what happens when a Three focuses too much on *talking* about how great they are – others usually do not receive this well and the Three's goal is not achieved. However, it is easy to truly be in awe of a Three who has a focus on action. An action-oriented Three's combination of motivation, charisma, and success places them in the perfect position to be leaders and role models. When you think of Oprah, a famous Three, what words come to mind? Our friends said: wise, generous, intelligent, and classy. Oprah's inherent drive to be the best, coupled with her desire to enrich the lives of others, has fashioned her into a force that has shaped millions of lives for the better.

Threes can do tremendous amounts of good with their natural drive and ambition, but this comes at no cost to their self-image. When Oprah created a magazine, she named it after her own first initial and made herself the cover model. Almost 20 years and 400 magazine covers later, you can still find Oprah gracing the front page of every single edition.

If you are a Three, you know that the relentless pursuit of success has its cost. On the one hand, it can serve to burn you out. While most people are happy to settle for "good enough," your need to be first means you have to aim higher, work harder, and never stop until the job is done. This can take its toll, as it often requires more effort and energy than you have at your disposal. The result is that you feel stressed, overstretched, and constantly concerned about potential failure. Remember to be kind to yourself every now and again. You are wired for success, and it will come. In moments when you feel your accomplishments are not being recognized, remember that the people you seek validation from are just people, just like you. The praise that comes from your own internal self-talk is just as valid, if not more valid, than the praise that comes from others. Remember that you are, and will always be, an achiever at your very core.

Chapter 4: The Individualist and Romantic

The fourth personality type in the Enneagram is often called the "Individualist," the "Romantic," or the "Four." This Enneatype stands in sharp contrast to Achievers as it is about self-perception rather than validation. Overall, a person in this type will be wholly focused on their identity, specifically as it relates to their emotional state. Subsequently, Fours will spend much of their time in their own minds, contemplating their thoughts, their feelings, and their need to express the rich content of their inner world. Such a need for self-expression leads many Fours to artistic lifestyles, providing the world with some of the best artists, musicians, designers, and poets. A common downside to the Four is their tendency to appear withdrawn and self-absorbed. Alternatively, one of the benefits of this personality type is the rich imagination a Four possesses, which often leads to some of the most meaningful conversations and experiences you could ever hope to have.

The Four in action

Markus is a recent high school graduate preparing to attend college and study to eventually become a lawyer. He excelled in high school, managing to attain straight A's while also participating in extra-curricular activities, like painting and theatre. Since he enjoys writing, he decides to major in English as a stepping-stone to law, which pleases his father, who thinks Markus would make a fantastic lawyer. As expected, Markus' first year is a success. His friends are in awe of his ability to pass his classes with ease, take on leadership positions in student groups, and attend parties and social events on the weekends. Markus is also very pleased with the start of college. His teachers seem to love his creative writing and critical assessments. He was also warmly welcomed onto the writing staff for the school news bulletin—a feat most freshmen are not able to accomplish.

As Markus progresses through his sophomore and junior classes, however, things start to shift. His advisors mandate that he takes more law-focused courses, leaving him with less time to pursue writing classes. He also has less time to write for the news bulletin, and his reputation morphs from being the prodigious freshmen wonderchild to the overworked junior with no time to create quality pieces. Markus' new professors do not appreciate his writing style and believe he needs to conform to standard legal writing practices if he is to succeed. He tries to cut down on "flowery language," as his professors call it, but still maintain a sliver of creativity that makes his work unique. He finds, however, that he is only able to maintain his high grades when he eliminates his creative flair almost completely. Markus grows bored of the day-to-day rut he now finds himself in and sinks into depression.

In April of Markus' junior year, Markus' parents, Sophie and Peter, notice that he has barely left his room. They knock on his door to speak with him and find him surrounded by canvases—each with the beginnings of collages assembled with remnants from his legal textbooks. Markus explains that he has stopped attending school two weeks prior and was working on a project that he would soon showcase in the hallways of the school. After this pop-up exhibition, he would formally drop-out to pursue art full-time.

Markus' father, Peter, does not understand this newfound passion, and thus is very much against his son's wishes to stop pursuing a career in law. Markus is unwilling to agree to his father's demands, choosing instead to follow his heart wherever it may lead. His mother, Sophie, understands both sides and thus is focused on trying to get father and son to reach some kind of agreement.

As a Four, Markus needs to live his life on his terms. Furthermore, he needs to live a life in which his individualism can thrive. Markus was happy and healthy when he had the space to thrive creatively and express himself, but once others stopped appreciating the specific elements that made him unique, he spiraled into a depression. Art allows Markus to express the rich inner world of his emotions, while also allowing him to be free from any rules that would restrict his imagination or expression. In contrast, Peter sees little value in such a life. As a Five, Peter sees emotions and self-expression as inferior qualities, choosing a life of intellectual prowess instead. He cannot understand his son's view of life, nor the values he places on non-intellectual concepts such as imagination and art. Sophie, being a Nine, sees the value in both arguments. Like most mothers, all she wants is for everyone to be happy, despite the fact that such a scenario is highly unlikely. Nevertheless, she will do what she can to bring both sides to a reasonable compromise.

The biggest lesson here is to recognize that Fours cannot be expected to follow anyone else's footsteps, no matter where those steps might lead. It's not about being an artist or a lawyer, rather it's about being able to pursue life with a free heart and an open mind. Furthermore, a Five will have a very different values system and definition of success. While Peter would see prestige and financial security as success, Markus would see the life of a starving artist as a success, provided it meant he was true to his heart and free to explore his passions.

Personality profile of the Four

Fours are referred to as Individualists because they desire to be unique and they love when others can see and appreciate their uniqueness. In fact, life for them is all about connecting to their true, individual selves and connecting with the specific traits that make them special. Fours desire to be different, but also want others to understand them. These desires can conflict with one another because often, when someone is different from everyone else, others do not readily understand them. Additionally, if a Four feels that they are too easily understood, they may begin to question whether they are truly unique.

The result of being unique often undermines a Four's other desire to feel as though they belong. The simple truth is that Fours are very emotional, meaning that they need to feel love and acceptance. This creates quite the conundrum as Fours usually shun the normal forms of entertainment and interaction that most of society engages in. Nevertheless, the aloof nature of the Four conceals a deep need for companionship and meaningful relationships. Since emotions are a vital part of their mindset, Fours tend to avoid superficial relationships, seeking only those of true depth and scope.

As part of the heart triad, Fours grapple with issues surrounding their self-image. Specifically, they have an idea of what their true self should look like (who they are at their "core" or within their "heart"), and work towards achieving unity with that image of themselves. They are driven by the need to understand their true selves and to be understood by others, in all their complexity. Fours quest to truly understand themselves and their unique attributes by digging deep into their core emotions. This makes Fours the Enneatype most comfortable with their emotions, as they allow themselves to fully feel both positive and negative emotions. Since Fours are practiced in exploring all types of emotions, they tend to find meaning in happenings that others take for granted. This can include events as simple as a casual glance, a laugh, or a sunset. Others may walk passed a sunset and think nothing of it, while a Four is more likely to be struck with emotion and seek out ways to express that emotion.

Fours often look to represent their purpose and contribution in a way that directly reflects their unique selves. They have an innate creativity that stems from their imaginative capacity – they can create whole worlds in their heads. Fours often enjoy the arts very much. They are always seeking inspiration and symbolism which further extends to their love of the arts. They can sometimes be actual artists, such as painters, actors, or musicians, but they don't have to be – their hallmark of creativity can be found in every field. Fours have their own unique view of the world and want to communicate it. They often use their creativity to illustrate their feelings, which can range anywhere from being ecstatic to feeling depressed. A healthy Four is very passionate and often has a high creative output.

Fours have several gifts due to their emotional connectivity. For one, they are usually emotionally courageous. They don't shy away from the ugly and difficult feelings life throws at us all, because they consider these emotions to be just as valuable as all others. Emotions are valuable to Fours because such feelings unite them with their core selves – the true identity they are always aiming to connect with. Fours can feel a bit melancholy, even on their good days, which sometimes makes others perceive them as negative, or melodramatic, people. This, however, is usually not the case. While people of other Enneatypes may push away and repress feelings of sadness, Fours accept them as they are in order to be as authentic as possible. The Four's wide range of emotional expressivity means they are not only able to feel sadness more than others can, but they can also see the beauty in life more easily, especially as it relates to their inner being. Emotional connectivity also drives the Four to seek pleasurable emotions. Some Fours even have a tendency for excessive self-indulgence – particularly during difficult times. Rather than seeing it as a flaw, Fours see this indulgent behavior as a restoration of balance. When deprived of pleasure due to overly stressful times, a Four might compensate by indulging in food, drink, shopping, and other forms of entertainment. They believe that life is to be enjoyed and so they seek pleasure in all things. Fours accept both the highs and lows of the human experience, making them the most romantic personality types on the Enneagram.

Another strength of the Four is in charting their own path. They are creative about their life paths and won't necessarily go with the flow. They are not afraid to question society's norms and do things a different way, because they want to do it *authentically*. They want to live their lives as an expression of their unique soul. For this reason, they do not succumb to peer pressure, either. Fours enjoy exploring the deeper aspects of their lives to make the changes they feel will make them happy, and make their outer life better reflect their inner life. The Four is a designer of their own life, often trying different jobs, activities, looks, partners, friendship groups, and hobbies on for size, in order to find the one that makes them feel most 'at home.'

Fours are not content to put on a mask as an identity; they want to get to the core of themselves and then reflect that outward into the world. As this takes a great deal of time, soul searching, and uncertainty, Fours can feel unsettled that others seem to know who they are so easily. This can cause a Four to believe they lack something that others may possess – whether that be the perfect relationship, the perfect body, or some other accomplishment. When the Four feels they cannot identify or connect with their true self, they may grow envious of the strong sense of self others appear to gain from their possessions or accomplishments. Among Fours, envy usually does not arise because they feel badly toward others or wish them ill, instead, it arises because they feel like they themselves fall short. When a Four's sense of self is particularly unstable, they can be quick to believe any negativity they hear about themselves. This can hurt deeply; but if a Four focuses on building their own self-esteem, they can learn to overlook negative words from others and grow increasingly secure with their own identity.

As Fours use their emotions to navigate themselves and the world in order to find their true identity, they gain high emotional awareness and sensitivity. They are very sensitive, highly instinctive, compassionate, empathetic, and emotionally complex. They develop the ability to pick up on other people's emotions, as well as their own. They not only want to find their true identity, they want others to find theirs, too. They always want to have emotionally charged and meaningful experiences – 'deep' conversations and relationships are their lifeblood. Fours are referred to as Romantics because of their ability to 'see' others and their longing to be seen themselves makes them truly romantic people. They try to tap into other people's core selves, and dislike phonies, small talk, and 'social masks'. Having an understanding of deep emotions helps Fours to create greater bonds with others and open up to others on a greater level. Despite their sensitivity, Fours are highly resilient and emotionally strong. They generally treat others with kind-heartedness, diplomacy, tenderness, and discretion.

Due to the fact that Fours value being unique and making special contributions, they tend to seek out careers that allow them the space to do so. This helps them to carve out their own specialized niches. Among Fours, you find experts in all kinds of niche subjects. When a Four has mastery over something, even if it is a very particular domain, this tends to increase their self-esteem. Fours tend to gravitate toward careers including advisor, teacher, librarian, social worker, counsellor, nutritionist, and personal trainer, to name a few. They love professions where they can teach, share emotions, show expertise, be their unique selves, and forge deep connections. Many choose to follow an artistic path.

Take, for example, Johnny Depp, a particularly famous Four. He's certainly not shy about charting his own path. He's taken on numerous roles – some quite unusual – and made himself a success across them all. He seems to be a sensitive soul who is guided by his feelings. He is also soft spoken and has an endearing quality about him. Depp has also been known to be rebellious yet compassionate – a typical Type Four.

If you know a Four, you may notice that they view themselves as different from everyone else. The idea of being different can be optimistic if the Four believes they are better than others, or pessimistic if the Four believes they are beneath others. Depending on where the Four in your life falls on this spectrum, you may experience them as either condescending and self-absorbed or self-deprecating and morose. As with most personality traits, the key to success is balance. Thus, healthy Fours will be able to identify several traits that make them unique, without a bias to focus on negative or positive aspects.

If you are a Four, remember that each intense emotion you feel is part of the ride that is life. These emotions may fluctuate often, but they never need to consume you. Your ability to feel more deeply than others equips you with the gift to see what others cannot and experience what others never will. You can channel these gifts into art so that others can better understand your perspective, but do not be too attached to ensuring that others comprehend everything about you. You are a unique human being with strengths, talents, and a soul that others cannot fully grasp. Even if you are currently on a quest to connect with your truest self, also remember to accept and value the person you are right now. You will always be special, without even having to try.

Part III: The Head Triad

Chapter 5: The Observer and Investigator

The fifth personality type on the Enneagram is often called the "Observer," the "Investigator," or the "Five." Fives, like Fours, are usually quite withdrawn and introverted. However, unlike Fours, the Five's inner world is one of intellect rather than emotion. Fives thrive on observing life from a safe distance. As a result, many choose occupations where they can apply their mental faculties in the safety of solitude and serenity. These include professions such as researchers, scientists, academics, and occasionally artists. Unfortunately, Fives often feel out of their depth in regular day-to-day life, seeing the hustle and bustle of the world as chaos that is likely to consume them. As a result, they tend to keep to themselves, leaving socializing and standard interaction for the more bold of heart. This isn't to say that they are incapable of having significant relationships, rather it simply means that such relationships must exist within their safe space and on their terms.

The Five in action

Peter works as a Math teacher at the local elementary school. His students have adored him from the moment he joined the teaching staff one year ago. Students complained that the last teacher was "boring." Peter, on the other hand, lit up when he discussed simple mathematical concepts and his enthusiasm infected his students. Students who failed math under the previous teacher were now flourishing, and in a survey that is conducted each year, 45% more students now report that math is their favorite subject.

As the current year comes to a close, Peter, his students, and their parents all prepare for the annual parent-teacher conference. Parents cycle from classroom-to-classroom to listen to a short presentation given by each teacher, and then briefly meet with the teacher one-on-one to discuss the specifics of their child.

When standing in front of a group of parents, Peter's face lit up—however this time, it was not with the joy and enthusiasm he usually feels when teaching. Instead, his face turned bright red. He looked down as he delivered his notes from several index cards that he shuffled between.

After the one-on-one meetings, a group of parents gathered outside the classroom to discuss. They were a bit confused. Peter seemed perfectly nice, but he was nothing like the person their kids described. Their kids described someone who was confident, knowledgeable, vibrant, and well-spoken. To them, Peter seemed quiet, timid, and uninspiring.

Why does Peter seem to have two completely different personalities? As a Five, Peter is quite introverted and enjoys learning and knowledge far more than he enjoys meeting and mingling with new people. In the safe space of his math classroom, he thrives. He could ramble about math concepts all day and teaching gives him the opportunity to do just that. Since he has known his students for several months now, he feels very comfortable with them, and can easily let his guard down to speak freely about math when around them. Meeting their parents, however, was another story entirely, especially since he was not supposed to speak to them about math. Peter felt uncomfortable in this scenario and found it difficult to put his best foot forward.

Personality profile of the Five

Fives are the observers, the thinkers, and the innovators. They are independent, objective, and analytical individuals. They try to have their own personal space where they can cultivate their knowledge, think, and enjoy silence. Fives are very rational people who study and observe everything that happens around them in great detail. They constantly examine reality. They desire to understand everything because understanding gives them a sense of calm. Therefore, they love knowledge and insight and are constantly on a journey of learning. Science is very important in their lives as they attempt to perceive the world through reason. They dislike things that distract their focus and enjoy private time where they can just be with their thoughts and ideas.

Fives are generally very intelligent and capable of understanding complex concepts. They thrive on being in their minds, do not become frustrated when approaching difficult concepts, and welcome opportunities to think through hard problems and mentally peel away their layers. This makes them very capable in any area where large amounts of research, study, or observation is required. In a way, Fives can be thought of as priests, with logic and intellectualism being their religion. They may cloister themselves away in the sacred spaces of libraries, academic institutions, and scientific laboratories where they can devote all of their energies to intellectual pursuits.

Fives, however, do not always pursue careers in academic fields. This is a common misconception that arises since Fives are the most cerebral of all the Enneatypes. A Five's tendency to collect information can manifest in his or her hobbies. Do you have a friend who seems to always be buried in a book? If so, your friend may be a Five. Perhaps your friend does not collect information on *all* topics but is extremely learned in one or two niches. A Five might focus in on particular niches and consume all possible information related to those topics in order to achieve a high level of mastery in those areas. No one has enough time to collect information on all subjects, but if a Five develops a fondness for sailboats, achieving mastery on sailboats may be enough to foster a sense of inner peace.

Fives are part of the head center, which consists of the Enneatypes that garner a sense of security through thinking and logic. A Five may feel uncomfortable taking action in the real world until they have retreated into their mind to dissect the situation and ensure they understand it thoroughly. Understanding breeds security, but unfortunately, not all situations can be understood fully. Even when a Five cannot achieve the level of understanding they desire, they may continue the quest and retreat farther and farther into their own mind, rejecting outside support and leaning heavily on overthinking. Does this mean that our sailboat enthusiast is uncomfortable taking action regarding sailboats? Is that why he collects so much information on sailboats? No, not necessarily. Our enthusiast friend may never see a real sailboat in his life. Even still, achieving mastery in the area of sailboats fosters an overall sense of security and inner peace that empowers him in other situations where he may feel uncomfortable. If our enthusiast friend begins to reject social events and reaches a pathological level of obsession with researching sailboats, it most likely reflects anxiety surrounding another area of life – anxiety that is alleviated with the acquisition of knowledge.

The Five's focus on collecting information and tendency to retreat internally leads to an introverted predisposition. While people of other Enneatypes are often swayed by emotions, a Five will usually value objectivity over subjectivity and push emotions out of the equation when assessing a situation. Emotions, after all, usually have little to do with the data, and a Five wants the data. A constant demand for objectivity leaves little room for developing emotional intelligence. Without emotional intelligence, a person cannot successfully interact with others. Some Fives purposefully reject relationships and are sufficiently satisfied engaging with their own thoughts. Other Fives desire relationships, but do not have the social skills to maintain them. These Fives find it hard to reduce the distance they put between themselves and others, but when they do, they are often devoted friends and long-lived companions.

Due to their emotional detachment, Fives often seem emotionally unexpressive even when they have strong feelings in their inner world. This can be most unfortunate as Fives often have a great deal of emotional response to any given situation. The problem isn't a lack of emotions, rather it's focus on logic and intellect that breeds unfamiliarity with (and sometimes even fear of) emotional expression. More often than not, when a person predominantly uses one side of their brain, it comes at the expense of the other. Thus, while a Five can solve complex problems and wrap their mind around concepts that would overwhelm the average person, that same Five may have never learned how to cope with and express their feelings. However, those who are privileged to get to know a Five well will often discover that they have a depth of emotion that is eager to be shared.

The difference between a healthy and unhealthy Five is the degree of willingness to interact and emotionally connect with others. In one unhealthy status, a Five may completely isolate due to fear of the outside world and a belief that they are only safe in their own mind. An unhealthy Five may also choose to isolate if they feel superior to others. In this case, they adopt an attitude of intellectual arrogance and judge other people according to what those people know or don't know. These unhealthy Fives appear contentious, withdrawn, and negative. When Fives are healthy, they become visionaries who have a rich and objective understanding of the world.

Objectivity is the Five's superpower. While others are getting bogged down in details and emotions, the Five can assess situations from a logical standpoint and sift through distractions that would derail others. This means that the Five can take in large amounts of data and distill it all down into nuggets the rest of the world can understand. Since Fives are not restricted to single perspectives ladled with emotional attachments, they can think outside the box more easily than others and see solutions and innovations that no one else can. Among the list of famous Fives, we can name Albert Einstein, who is considered the most renowned scientist of the 20th century; John Lennon, who left a mark as a musician, pacifist, composer, writer, and a leader of one of the most iconic rock bands of all times; Stephen Hawkings, who was an extraordinary physicist, theoretician, cosmologist, and science researcher who worked on the basic laws that govern the universe; and

Bill Gates, the cofounder of Microsoft. Fives in their best state maintain a balance between interacting with the world and withdrawing from it. This balance of behavior is often associated with wisdom and intellectual genius. Healthy Fives actively offer the world the fruit of their knowledge, often through teaching and writing, but they could also be great musicians or excel in one of the many sciences. Whatever they do, healthy Fives look for areas where their talents and knowledge can impact something beyond themselves.

If you are a Five, you may feel tempted to focus exclusively on the inner monologue of your thoughts, but there is also value in connecting to yourself physically. It is helpful to move your body (through dance, sports, etc) and pay attention to your bodily sensations in order to anchor yourself in your physical body as well as the external. To have internal balance, you must have external balance. Balance between your internal and external worlds is the key that will fashion your talents of knowledge and understanding into a tool that will contribute valuable insights to the world.

Chapter 6: The Loyalist and Skeptic

The sixth personality type on the Enneagram is often called the "Loyalist," the "Skeptic," or the "Six." This is one of the hardest types to identify as those belonging to it are nothing short of a contradiction. For the most part, Sixes strive to find a person or cause to commit themselves to. In this way they can be highly valuable assets, providing the support, devotion, and energy that keep things moving along. However, underneath this need to be loyal is a suspicion of people and their motives. This means that Sixes are as likely to be rebellious as they are to be devoted, which makes them the most confusing of all Enneagram types. Fortunately, when you know how to properly relate with a Six, you can gain a friend of immeasurable value – one that will remain with you until the end.

The Six in action

Jane and Dana are assistant managers at Café Fresh. One of their new bosses from headquarters, Henry, has asked them to implement a revamped training protocol when working with the newly hired baristas. Jane loves the idea behind the vision and is excited to get to work. In a meeting with Henry and Dana, however, Jane begins to grow more worried than excited. Henry had a general idea of what he wanted the training to look like, but he didn't have concrete answers to all of Jane's questions about what to do if she was thrown curveballs during the training sessions. Jane thought Dana would share in her frustration, but Dana looked unfazed during the meeting and didn't seem to have any questions at all.

After the meeting, Jane spoke to Dana about the situation and asked her how she could be calm in the face of so much ambiguity. Dana reassured her that the new training was "no big deal," that she thought Henry was just trying to make a name for himself at headquarters, and that everyone would forget about the new training plan in a couple of weeks. Since the higher-ups barely visited the cafes and would almost certainly never attend a barista training session, Dana planned to continue the curriculum that has worked for them for the last four years that they've been assistant managers. Jane agreed that Henry would never know if they adopted the new curriculum, but also thinks they must have put him in charge for a reason. Headquarters likely conducted research to decide on which training system would be best. Plus, Henry seems like a great boss with potential to make their café better, so it would probably be best to trust his vision. Jane decides that she will try to use the new curriculum, but still needs to figure out what to do about all the potential areas where problems might arise.

Jane eventually decided to take it upon herself to draft up a plan of action that includes responses to issues that might arise during the revamped training. She then sent the plan to Henry so he could give it a quick approval – this way, if a problem arose in the middle of a training session, she wouldn't be left unsure of what the appropriate response should be.

Henry appreciated this initiative and met with Jane to hash out the details of what would work and what would not work. Together, they finalized a plan that included the core curriculum as well as instructions on what to do if the training took unexpected turns. At the end of this, both Jane and Henry were satisfied.

As a Type Six, Jane had trouble wrapping her mind around the idea of ignoring an authority figure who she respected. She responded very positively to Henry's guiding ideas and wanted to align her actions with the new system he was proposing. Even when it was brought to her attention that the old system had been working fine, she remained loyal to this new idea that she now believed in. Staying true to the idea alone, however, was not enough to put Jane at ease, as she began thinking up ways in which things could go wrong. She noticed the cracks in the new system that might leave her unsupported and needed to close those potential pitfalls before she felt truly secure. Since Henry is a Type One, he did not anticipate all of the same issues that Jane did, but he was happy when she brought them to his attention and they could work through the issues together.

Personality profile of the Six

Sixes secured the nickname of "Loyalists" because they are the Enneatype most loyal to their friends, family, and beliefs. Their loyalty results from a desire to give support as a means to secure support from other people in return. If they are loyal to friends and family, they expect that those friends and family members will reciprocate with love, care, and devotion. The Six's greatest fear is often that they will be left without support or guidance, and thus, they value security and safety more than anything else. You may be thinking: "Don't all people want love and support? Is this personality trait truly specific to the Enneagram Type Six?" Yes, love is a basic human need — there's no doubt about that. However, for the Six, the need for external support is so critical that it is the core motivation for many of their thoughts and actions. Above all else, Sixes desire to be safe, feel supported by others, and have certainty and tranquility.

Sixes are part of the head center because of their tendency to think their way through life. To ensure that they and their loved ones are safe at all times, Sixes develop the ability to foresee challenges, anticipate problems, and think of all the possible solutions. Sixes value seeing situations from all angles, because if they understand all of the nuances of an entity, then they can come to a firm decision on whether that entity is secure enough to be trusted. We saw this when we met Jane, who seemed to think through Henry's new idea more than Henry himself even could. Jane wanted to trust Henry and his new plan, but could not fully do so until she gained a thorough understanding of the plan itself, as well as all of the exceptions to the plan. Then, and only then, she felt confident in the plan and eager to devote herself to its implementation.

Jane also demonstrated another trait shared by many Sixes: the desire for external guidance. She could have drafted the report to her own satisfaction and left Henry out of the picture. Sixes, however, often doubt their own judgments. This stems from deeply rooted insecurity and manifests as anxiety and a constant search for external guidance or validation. Sixes often fulfill this desire for guidance by finding institutions and systems that they can trust. Sixes tend to be dedicated supporters of the organizations that form their community. When the available institutions are lacking, they have the tendency to devote time and effort to improving upon them. If there are no organizations present, they will likely devote time to developing them from the ground-up. Sixes resist disorganization and often require that elements in their lives must be systematized to ensure that everything works together in an efficient method. This is because organization and efficiency are qualities that make for a system that can offer support even in the face of unexpected mishaps. To ensure that their institutions offer sufficient security, Sixes often become community leaders who forge strong alliances and bonds to bring about cooperation. They are able to champion a cause and inspire people to join in on that cause. Just as Sixes are loyal to their friends and family, they also have the tendency to be loyal to their institutions and beliefs as well. They will usually ask several questions before making the leap to fully commit; however, once they make up their mind about something that they believe in, they will defend their belief at all costs.

Many believe that the Six is the most prevalent personality type on the Enneagram, with some estimating that up to 50% of people are Enneatype Six. This large group, however, can be broken down into two varieties: the phobic and the counter-phobic Six. So far, we've discussed the qualities that make a Six feel the most comfortable — safety, security, love, and devotion. What happens when a Six feels that their security and love are being threatened? When threatened, someone might try to avoid the person or thing at the source of the threat, or they might face it head-on and try to out-threaten the threat itself. This distinction is what separates the phobic and counter-phobic Sixes. Phobic Sixes tend to respond to fear by becoming fearful. They adopt an attitude of vigilance — scanning the environment and looking for ways to create safety and escape from the threat. On the other hand, counter-phobic Sixes are afraid of the very feeling of being afraid and chase away their own fear by standing up to the source. Counter-phobic Sixes are often defiant and rebellious. Despite this attitude, they are very loyal and idealistic people. We see the pinnacle of loyalty meets counter-phobia when studying the atrocities that occurred in

Nazi Germany. Nazis were devoted to their cause and united in an effort to stand-up to people who they deemed to be a threat. Thankfully, the majority of Sixes, whether phobic or counter-phobic, will not reach this type of extreme. In the general population, counter-phobic Sixes will simply move towards what makes them afraid, while phobic Sixes will move away from what makes them afraid.

When discussing the Enneagram Type Six, the word "anxiety" arises often. Anxiety, however, does not necessarily need to sit in the control seat of every Six's life. Sixes can grow to a better path free from anxiety and fear when they recognize that the only real security in life comes from within. While they can work hard to build their finances, to find the right friends and the right partner, to foresee any possible mishap, etc, ultimately, none of the external structures they use to give them confidence will ever lead to complete security. Life is inherently flawed, which means that nothing can be completely controlled. Things will always go wrong, and support systems will change. Therefore, a Six's growth depends on their ability to find support in their own internal knowledge. It is about finding the place within themselves that is calm, strong, and capable.

If you are a Six, your family and friends know that you are the person they can always rely on because 1) your unparalleled loyalty sets you apart from all other people and 2) you naturally think of solutions to problems that others haven't even identified as problems yet. Your devotion to others and outward focus makes you an excellent team member when working alongside others or a team leader who is always one step ahead of the group. Remember that the balance of external and internal guidance is key. You can reap the most reward when you marry your ability to foresee events that may happen in the future with a deep trust in your ability to handle those future events. Trust yourself, and others will trust you.

Chapter 7: The Enthusiast

The seventh personality type on the Enneagram is often called the "Enthusiast" or the "Seven." This personality type is largely defined by an eager and never-ending search for pleasure and distraction. Sevens can be misidentified as Threes as a result of their high energy and extroverted approach to life. Additionally, their constant state of planning can be misconstrued for genuine goals and ambitions. The main difference between Sevens and Threes, however, is that Sevens often lack the finished product. Rather than achievement, it is excitement and adventure that inspires Sevens to action. Once the excitement is gone, they change course — seeking their next rush of adrenaline.

The Seven in action

Dirk is an English teacher at the local elementary school. He started working at the school one year ago and is delighted to be surprised with a party to celebrate his teaching anniversary. He is sharing the party with Peter, who also started working at the school one year ago, so Dirk drapes his arm across Peters' shoulders while he makes rounds to thank all the other teachers and staff for coming to the party. Dirk is the kind of person who lights up the room when he speaks. He would probably be just as friendly and talkative if this was not even his party. In his classroom, no lecture is the same — he comes up with exciting new ways to present each novel his students read. He brings this same energy to social scenarios like this one, where he easily engages everyone in conversation, facilitates introductions between others, and brings a sense of calm and laughter to those he speaks with.

Halfway through the party, Dirk thinks it would be a great time for a toast. He once again grabs Peter and tries to get everyone's attention. While he's doing this, Peter mentions to Dirk that he actually does not want to be in the spotlight, because it would add to his anxiety. Confused, Dirk asks Peter what's going on, and Peter admits to being stressed about a couple of things going on at home. Dirk immediately understands where Peter is coming from and remembers his own difficulties at home. Two weeks ago, his wife told him that she's been feeling neglected and wants a divorce. Dirk flashes a smile at Peter and pours him more wine, hoping to bring him some comfort. He then resumes to getting the room's attention and gives a heartfelt speech about how happy he has been to work among the people surrounding him. Everyone seemed to enjoy the speech; they chuckled amongst themselves occasionally, and at one point, someone even yelled out "aww we love you too Dirk!" Dirk loved the feeling this gave him and wanted Peter to feel the same rush. He handed the mic to Peter and motioned for him to give a speech of his own. Peter's face turned bright red and everyone started chanting "Speech! Speech! Speech!" Peter was frozen for a few seconds, but Dirk leaned over and whispered some encouraging words in his ears. Peter immediately loosened up, smiled, and said a few words into the mic. Everyone clapped, and the two smiled as mingling continued.

Dirk turned to Peter afterward saying: "I knew you had it in you! Doesn't it feel great?" Peter, however, was frowning. He reminded Dirk that he did *not* want the spotlight on him and that it only added to his anxiety. Dirk was confused.

Everyone loved Peter's speech, and Peter even seemed happy while doing it. Dirk explained that he just wanted Peter to reach his full potential and feel the same rush he did. In the midst of all the excitement, Dirk had not considered that Peter might not want the spotlight on him. Peter started to grow angry since he had just told Dirk that he did not want excess attention and started to wonder if Dirk was even listening when he spoke. Unable to resolve the conflict, the two parted and continued their mingling separately.

In this scenario, problems arose because of differences in how Dirk, a Seven, and Peter, a Five, gain energy and peace of mind. Dirk is an extrovert who loves the spotlight. Dirk also has a tendency to deal with conflict by ignoring the issue and focusing on exciting activities that distracts from negativity. Since Dirk loves the sense of adventure and excitement, it is difficult for him to understand why others do not like it when he refuses to focus on their pain and instead, tries to counteract that pain with joy. Dirk did not ignore Peter's request because he does not care about Peter. On the contrary, he truly wanted Peter to feel good, but did not realize that the actions that makes him feel good are not the same actions that would make Peter feel good. At the end of the day, Dirk simply wanted to spread joy to everyone at the party, including himself and Peter.

Personality profile of the Seven

Sevens are oriented towards freedom, experience, and positivity. As a group, they are the most optimistic, adventurous, and fun-loving people on the Enneagram. They tend to make their lives an exciting adventure, so they are always in search of having many different experiences. Sevens value a sense of freedom and focus on optimism, being inspired, being playful and spontaneous, and taking opportunities as they present themselves. The Seven's virtue of optimism and hope is a fundamental quality that makes it easy for them to enjoy life and make others enjoy themselves. When we met Dirk, he was the soul of the party, making everybody laugh at his jokes and bringing joy, cheer, and pleasure to all the people who were there.

As Sevens are always looking for new and exciting experiences, they are future-oriented people who are generally convinced that something better is just around the corner. Subsequently, they have a tendency to dream up a future that promises new and better events. They are fast thinkers who have a lot of energy, so they can often be found making a lot of plans. Many people who have a dream struggle with starting the process of chasing that dream. Sevens can be very beneficial when it comes to providing the spark for a new project or endeavor. They can help to provide the impetus to get the ball rolling in even the most challenging of pursuits. Sevens tend to be outgoing, talented, creative, and open-minded. They are practical people who have multiple abilities. They know how to move through social networks and promote their interests. They often have an entrepreneurial spirit and are able to convey their enthusiasm to the people around them. Therefore, their main strength is to see the best in others and to inspire others to achieve their full potential.

The Seven's eagerness to chase new, bigger, and brighter experiences can become problematic if they are never content with what they have. Sevens who are prone to pursue one dream after another rarely stay the course long enough to see the dream realized. Instead, once the excitement of the quest diminishes, they seek out new challenges to rekindle their adventurous spirit. The endless search of new things and experiences can also lead Sevens to find it hard to make constant efforts over time to achieve their objectives. Since Sevens often dislike being idle, they may fear missing out on experiences and gravitate towards trying everything they can. For this reason, focusing does not come easily for Sevens, and the tendency to believe that something better is going to turn up in the horizon makes them reluctant to narrow down their options or to pursue their aims with true devotion. As a result, Sevens may run out of time and find they cannot explore everything they desire since there will always be something they cannot reach. If this happens, Sevens can start to feel frustrated and impatient with themselves and develop a bitter sense of non-fulfillment and disappointment.

As part of the head, or thinking, center, Sevens tend to quell their deep anxieties by keeping their mind occupied with thoughts on which activities they will complete next. They ensure that they will always feel pleasure with a (sometimes compulsive) search for new experiences. Such experiences distract from negative thoughts and can even lead to a complete disconnect with negative realities and emotions. In the face of uncomfortable emotions, unhealthy Sevens may direct their consciousness to something that makes them feel good. For example, if you have an uncomfortable conversation with a Seven, they may unknowingly forget completely, due to their tendency to escape problems by focusing on planning new activities and experiences. Even when a Seven is emotionally connected enough to recognize their discomfort, they may have difficulties focusing on the uncomfortable feelings and trying to work them out. Sevens frequently remember and define their childhood as happy, even if it wasn't that way. Sevens can ignore the negative aspects of their past, just like they can ignore the negative aspects of their day-to-day. They often look away from what makes them suffer. Dirk, for example, responded to the memory of his impending divorce by smiling bigger and giving a heartfelt speech that spread joy throughout the entire room. His positivity, laughter, jokes, and optimism were partially a mask to cover his fears and anxiety. He is in the middle of a hard and painful life change, and the best way he knows to escape from those thoughts is to become a joker and refuse to take himself too seriously.

Sevens make great friends and companions. However, when it comes to deep and meaningful relationships, they can be a bit complicated. Since they do not like to focus on their own pains and sorrows, they tend to dismiss the pains and sorrows of others. Rather than trying to solve a situation, they will choose to find a distraction, such as going to the movies, engaging in a competitive activity, or pursuing some other scenario which provides excitement, adventure, and the promise of glory. If you have a Seven in your life, the trick is to realize that their inability to recognize your emotional needs is simply due to the fact that they often ignore their own emotional needs. This behavior is usually not intentional and does not reflect their feelings towards you.

How can an unhealthy seven move towards a healthier status? They can become aware of whether and how they avoid negative experiences. No one can live without going through pain and frustration, because these are natural parts of life. If they avoid negative sensations, Sevens miss the opportunity of having the whole experience of life. Sevens can correct this by listening carefully to other people, suppressing their tendency to jump into action, and staying mindful and present in the current moment.

If you are a Seven, you have the unique ability to create positivity and joy out of thin air. This, coupled with your tendency to stay busy and chase big dreams, perfectly positions you to see hope when others cannot and lead others out of difficult situations. Remember that you do not need to ignore the negative to achieve the positive. In fact, you are the person most equipped to assess a negative situation and find the glimmer of hope that still exists there.

Part IV:
The Gut Triad

Chapter 8: The Challenger and Protector

The eighth personality type on the Enneagram is often called the "Challenger," the "Protector," or simply, the "Eight." People in this Enneatype display controlling personalities, which can be harmful when not kept in proper balance. Such controlling personalities cause Eights to seek either independence or dominance as they cannot accept being told what to do by others. Subsequently, they usually choose occupations where they can rise to prominent positions or where they can work alone, such as in freelance work. When it comes to relationships, Eights find it hard to let others into their personal lives, meaning that close relationships are few and far between. However, when Eights do allow someone into their heart, it provides for a wonderful and enduring experience that is well worth the wait.

The Eight in action

Dana is an assistant manager at Café Fresh alongside her colleague, Jane. The two of them are responsible for training the new baristas who join their team — like Markus, a college student hoping to earn money during his summer break. During a training session, Dana and Jane explain the dress code: all employees must wear khaki pants, a burgundy polo, and black shoes. Only natural hair tones are allowed, and excessive accessories or jewelry are discouraged. Markus, who has a streak of green hair and a lip ring, interjects to ask what is meant by 'excessive.' This question came as a surprise to Dana, because she was still in the middle of explaining the policy and did not yet open the section for questions. She pauses to regroup her thoughts and then turns to Markus to explain that 'excessive' refers to anything that differs from what the average person would consider to be workplace appropriate. She quickly scans him from top to bottom, and then tells him that he would need to change his look before orientation concludes if he would like to keep his job. Markus opens his mouth to ask a follow-up question, but he notices that Dana has already turned away to look back at her notes. The room falls silent as Dana reshuffles her papers to find her spot in the curriculum.

After the training, Markus pulls Jane aside to ask about the incident that occurred during training. He felt that Dana had snapped at him and was harsh when telling him his look was inappropriate, especially since she did it in front of all the other new baristas. In retrospect, he knows he could have waited for Dana to ask the group if anyone had questions, but he thought the way he interrupted Dana was quite gentle and did not warrant the snappy response he received. He wanted to be on Dana's good side, but was unsure of how to even begin to correct the situation. He was also a bit nervous that he would say the wrong thing if he tried to apologize directly to Dana. Thus, he asked Jane to intervene. Jane sighed. She, too, felt the tension after Dana responded to Markus. She explained to Markus that the event was simply Dana being Dana. In general, she is quite matter-of-fact in communicating when she feels something is out-of-place. Jane also cautioned Markus that he would receive similar responses if he ever interrupted Dana again. Jane herself makes a point not to do this, and even though she and Dana are technically equals, Dana ends up doing most of the talking and decision-making when they work together. This is because Jane has learned that their relationship runs a bit more smoothly if she allows Dana to take the reins in most scenarios.

As promised, Jane went to Dana and told her about the conversation with Markus. Dana was, again, shocked. She was annoyed that Markus interrupted her and wanted to immediately tell him off. Even when she repressed that desire to tell him off and gave him what she considered to be a calm response, Markus was still rubbed the wrong way. She was also surprised to hear that the room felt tense after she spoke. She thought her response was level-headed, accurate, and necessary.

In this scenario, Dana was put off by the 'new kid' challenging her authority by interrupting her while she was speaking. She did not express this anger directly with her words, but it was still felt by everyone in the room. As an Eight, Dana's instinct is to express her emotions as they arise, however, she knows that this type of response is not always the most effective. Thus, she makes an effort to refrain from expressing many of the emotions she feels. Still, others around her often feel the large energy she carries with her, especially when a passionate feeling is stirring within her.

Personality profile of the Eight

Eights are intense people who gravitate towards intense emotions. They have the strongest energy of all personality types on the Enneagram. They are strong-willed, self-confident, decisive, assertive, tenacious, and energetic. Eights enjoy taking on challenges in life and they have the physical and psychological capacity to persuade others to follow their lead — whether they are starting a new business or rebuilding a city. Eights have a motivational need to be strong and avoid showing vulnerability. So, they value having a sense of control and being direct and impactful. Therefore, they take action with great ease and are people who tackle confrontations head on. They want a lot out of life and feel fully prepared to go out, get it, and simultaneously protect themselves against anyone or anything that might derail their plans.

Eights are part of the gut or instinctual center, which consists of the Enneatypes led by their visceral reactions. Eights have ready access to their visceral feelings (especially feelings of anger) and can be quick to act on them. This often stems from an Eight's unconscious fear of being left vulnerable and taken advantage of. They tend to guard against this by quickly and passionately taking action to achieve their desired outcomes and, more importantly, identify and defend against any potential obstacles or roadblocks. Eights often take the stance that the best defense is a good offense.

Because Eights express their emotions quickly and intensely, their overall style can sometimes be perceived as aggressive — however, in many instances, society has given Eights the message that their natural style is unacceptable, and so Eights learn to channel it into a more tamed version of themselves. When this happens, the Eight has condensed enormous amounts of energy into a very small package, and they will be felt as a large energetic presence when they enter a room. Enneatype Eight is a territorial character par excellence. Everyone can feel their strong presence because their action bias makes it easy for them to influence the external environment. They have no problem when projecting themselves as direct and intense, so it is almost impossible to not feel an Eight's presence wherever they are. This is likely to come across through the way they speak, their choice of words, decision-making style, and body language.

Since Eight radiate such large amounts of energy, they are natural leaders that others tend to respect and turn to when seeking guidance. They are authoritative and decisive, which gives them the ability to make things happen rather quickly. Eights earn respect through being honorable, using power constructively, defending others, and acting as a provider and promoter of noble causes. Though they dislike weakness and incompetence, Eights are often highly protective of people they feel responsible for. When people under their care are being exploited or treated unjustly, Eights will defend and protect them, as long as they don't act like victims. They will pursue justice and will actively work to correct wrongs.

Beneath the Eight's tough exterior is a layer of vulnerability. The Eight is not more or less vulnerable than any other person, but what separates them from others is their aversion to the idea of being controlled, disempowered, or exploited for their vulnerabilities. They do not like the idea of being hurt by anyone or anything, so they take strong measures to ensure that this will never happen. This means trust may not come easy for them, however, when an Eight does manage to trust someone, they find a firm ally and unconditional friend who they will relentlessly support and defend.

If you know an Eight, forming a deep and meaningful personal relationship may prove a daunting task. Since Eights value their autonomy and do not like to be controlled, the more you try to push a relationship is the more likely they will push you away. The best advice is to simply allow the Eight to come to you. If you present yourself as someone who does not waver due to the Eight's intense energy and does not allow life to knock you down, you will gain the

Eight's respect. Once you are welcomed into the Eight's heart, you can rest assured knowing that they will be very devoted to and protective of you.

Healthy Eights fight to get what they need and want, so they are oriented to action and have an attitude of "I can do it" – which comes from a great sense of internal motivation to act on their gut instincts to extract everything they can from life. This internal motivation is an offshoot of the passionate energy they feel for life, for justice, and for their ideals. They put passion in their discussions, in their affections, and in the ways they have fun. Therefore, they feel the most alive when they put intensity into everything they do. Healthy Eights use their immense strength to be sensitive to the needs of others and are aware of the way their actions impact those around them. They also allow others to help them and don't necessarily feel the need to always be in control. They are motivated by a strong sense to be at peace with the world and themselves, and they can balance their tremendous strength and desire to be in control with allowing others to see their vulnerability.

Unhealthy Eights are prone to anger. Their desire to control the environment and accrue power becomes corrupted by their own selfish interests. They over-identify with being strong as a way to deny their insecurities, often denying them so well that they even manage to lie to themselves. This is how an unhealthy Eight survives in a world that they consider to be dangerous and constantly issuing threats against them and their goals. They may go so far as to intimidate others and make them feel weak, just so they can look and feel strong in comparison.

The most unhealthy Eights seek confrontation at every opportunity and try to make contact with others mainly through disputes. They can be crude and brutal. From their point of view, the world is like a jungle where the strongest wins — and they do everything possible to win. Under this premise, they consider it reasonable to fight for their interests, dominate others, and demand that others conform to their will.

Eights are easy to identify by their decisive and strong-willed natures. They are the people who take the lead in any group, especially when the situation is difficult, or threatening. Possessing high levels of energy and pragmatism, Eights prove worthy leaders who quickly earn the respect and trust of those under their direction. Not given to emotional contemplations, Eights spend their energies finding logical and practical solutions to problems, making them ideal in business and military environments. Eights are bold, energetic individuals who possess the ability and desire to lead with vision and confidence. We find many Eights among the presidents and prime ministers of nations. Martin Luther King Junior is also a famous Eight who demonstrated numerous leadership qualities during his fight for equal rights over the course of history. He showed great courage during his lifetime by challenging the authority with his numerous protests and marches for the issues he believed so strongly in.

If you are an Eight, you understand what it takes to reach great heights and develop strength, tenacity, and resilience. You are unstoppable. Despite your unmatched power, however, you must avoid the trap of thinking that you can do everything yourself or that you don't need to rely on others. Expressing your weaknesses does not mean that you are weak, it means that you're human and living the best we know how. The world undoubtedly needs people like you to push the rest of us forward, because as an Eight, you have great power at your disposal: power of personality, physical power, and emotional power. Cultivate these powers well and you will ensure that your legacy is not one of intimidating force, but is one of admirable strength.

Chapter 9: The Peacemaker

The ninth personality type on the Enneagram is often referred to as the "Peacemaker" or the "Nine." People with this personality type are among the most friendly, easy-going, and harmonious people you will ever meet. They are also the ones who see the best in people, holding out faith that there is good in everyone no matter how bad a person's actions or behavior actually is. More often than not, however, Nines withdraw from society to a large degree, especially in the event of conflict or emotionally charged situations. This is because Nines cannot stand conflict or strife in any way, shape, or form. When they do interact with others, they prove trustworthy friends, reliable coworkers, and very likable in general.

The Nine in action

Sophie has spent the last week trying to come up with ideas to cheer up her son, Markus, who seems to be having a rough time in college. She asks her husband, Peter, what he thinks about getting Markus a dog. Peter says he will think about it, but does not bring the topic up again for weeks. After three weeks has passed, Sophie asks Peter what he thinks they should do about Markus. Peter suggests that they should all go on a family vacation together and asks Sophie to do some research on affordable weekend destinations. She happily agrees.

Two days later, Peter asks Sophie if she's started the research. She apologizes profusely, saying she completely forgot but would start right away. Another two days later, Peter asks again. This time, Sophie says she's been extremely busy helping her sister with a seasonal project. After a week goes by and Sophie has still not started the research, Peter asks her if everything is okay. She assures him that things are fine and that she plans to do the research soon. Peter tells her that he will do some digging on his own to help speed things up. By the end of the evening, he shows her a plan for the following weekend.

One week later, Markus, Peter, and Sophie pile into a car and drive to their weekend destination. The three have a relaxing and quiet evening, until Markus and Peter have a squabble over what to watch on television one evening. Sophie hears the disagreement from the other room and leaps up to intervene. She hears both sides of the argument and notices that the fight was not really about the television at all. Instead, Markus was feeling frustrated and was having trouble expressing that to his father. Peter did not pick up on this and thought Markus' behavior was simply rude. Sophie picked up the nuances of the situation immediately and was able to smooth out the situation with ease. The three spent several moments talking through the underlying concerns until they were all satisfied with the resolution.

As a Nine, Sophie is constantly on the lookout for ways to keep the peace. She can get each party to see the value of the other person's opinions and behaviors, and thus find common ground that they can both agree upon and eliminate conflict. Like many Nines, sometimes Sophie can be so preoccupied with the pursuit of peace, that she does not take a stand when her own needs are not being met. In this scenario, Sophie felt like Peter completely ignored her idea on how to best cheer Markus up, but instead of asking Peter about this directly, she allowed the idea to get swept under the rug. Rather than voicing her anger about this, she took the passive aggressive approach of ignoring Peter's request that she look up vacation destinations. By claiming she forgot or was too busy to complete the task, Sophie could still keep the peace and avoid admitting that she did not intend to do it because she was upset. In her pursuit of harmony, she did not make a big deal of her own feelings during the vacation, and instead focused her energies outward. This is why she, and many Nines, assume the role of the "peacemaker." Their affinity to dissolve conflict and passive demeanors equips Nines with the makeup to bring out a sense of ease and comfort in others.

Personality profile of the Nine

Nines are gentle, modest, and caring people by nature. They are motivated by a need to be settled and in harmony with the world, and so, they try to be as accommodating and accepting as possible. They strive for a peaceful existence, appreciate stability, and prefer to avoid conflict.

Not quick to judge, they will often forgive any wrongdoing in order to return to a peaceful coexistence free of stress and drama. Furthermore, they will tend to focus on the positives in any given situation to avoid issues that might rock the boat and upset the peace they crave.

Nines are part of the gut triad, which consists of the Enneatypes that are highly perceptive to their own bodies and primarily informed through their gut instincts. Nines specifically have an overwhelming desire to feel grounded in their bodies and feel physical harmony between their internal and external worlds. Put simply, Nines gravitate towards peace and avoid conflict. They often try to maximize the chance of peace by being easy-going, agreeable, and complacent to the point that they will often put other's needs ahead of their own. They tend to avoid animosity at all costs, whether it be internal or interpersonal. Their mantra is to go with the flow, which could lead to an extremely relaxed and tranquil existence, but could also cause unexpressed frustration if a Nine does not assert themselves when necessary. We saw this happen with Sophie, who had an opinion on what she and her husband should do to help their son through a rough time. When Sophie's opinion was ignored for three weeks, she did not bother to reassert her position and decided to go along with her husband's suggestion in order to avoid any type of tension. Perhaps Peter simply forgot that Sophie had made a suggestion of her own. If this were the case, he would never know his error since Sophie is unwilling to shine light on something that may lead to bickering. A Nine may remain calm and seemingly unfazed even after others wrong them, but if the Nine has not developed healthy mechanisms for coping with stressors, their frustration may build internally and present in unexpected ways. In Sophie's case, she expressed her upset with her husband by simply ignoring his request that she research vacation destinations. This is a passive aggressive approach to dealing with conflict that less healthy Nines often adopt. These Nines satisfy their need to be aggressive through the passive means of ignoring the situation, while maintaining their need for peace by refusing to tackle the problem head-on.

Unhealthy Nines often look happy and calm, but their stability is based more on denial than on genuine and conscious acceptance. They evade with routine activities, deny their emotions, and wait until the problems are resolved on their own – anything that doesn't involve actually facing a conflict. If problems do not disappear, they minimize them to appease others and to have peace at all costs. How can a Nine overcome this tendency to evade conflict? Opportunity for growth arises when Nines start to realize that ignoring a problem does not make it go away. They learn to defeat the habitual response of choosing the least problematic strategy, which may not necessarily be the best way to tackle an issue. Instead, they make the decision to stay present to the problem and actively seek out a solution.

Nines can also grow towards health by choosing to stand their ground, even when doing so might jeopardize the peace. Perhaps the greatest pitfall a Nine faces is being taken advantage of. Nines often overlook other people's faults and wrongdoings, being quick to forgive and forget. Unfortunately, this means that they will often allow others to mistreat them or take them for granted again and again – which can cause a significant amount of emotional turmoil. Nines may allow repeated offenses from others simply because they do not want to take actions that may lead to change – as any change, good or bad, will upset the status quo. Change, however, is not only inevitable, but is also necessary at times. Once a Nine realizes this, they can stop resisting change and try to facilitate it to restore balance even faster. Nines can also yield to change to prevent conflict from taking root in their hearts and minds, as accepting and adapting to newness is paramount to the pursuit of inner and outer peace.

At their core, a Nine's requirement for balance is ever-present, but individual mechanisms to try and maintain peace will differ depending on a Nine's particular level of health. The difference between healthy and unhealthy Nines can best be seen when harmony and balance are threatened. A healthy Nine will go out of their way to take action and restore the peace, while an unhealthy Nine will disconnect with their sensations to avoid feeling the sense of unbalance. In their best status, Nines feel internally tranquil and permeate everything that surrounds them with that tranquility. They have the ability to acknowledge and assess the full depth of difficult realities, but are simultaneously able to recognize that balance can often be restored, even in the face of life's challenges. They are available to listen to others and provide them with a relaxing and conciliatory point of view. They are natural facilitators of reconciliation and are very impartial in their judgments. They awaken confidence and affection, make people feel comfortable and at ease, and have a calming and healing influence. Healthy Nines harmonize groups and unite people. They understand that it is not necessary for them to ignore the challenges of life to maintain balance. Instead, they choose to accept challenges without losing their center or their sense of what is truly important. Nelson Mandela was a Civil rights activist, the first black president of South Africa, and the epitome of a healthy Nine. Mandela is a symbol of global peacemaking. He did not evade conflicts, but instead, faced problems with great firmness and a wealth of inner peace.

If you are a Nine, you were given the ability to bring harmony to the world. Once you recognize that true peace begins inside you, you can take that peace with you wherever you go. Remember that dark and difficult situations need not threaten the natural sense of calm you carry with you. You can acknowledge challenges, appropriately deal with them, and still maintain your serene nature. Your presence alone teaches those around you how they, too, can be happy with the simple things and remain optimistic in trying times. You can change the world by infecting it with the much-needed harmony that flows naturally from your core.

Chapter 10: The Reformer and Perfectionist

The first personality type on the Enneagram is often called the "Reformer," the "Perfectionist," or the "One." People with this personality type are idealists by nature. They tend to be very responsible in their actions and often appear more mature than their age. Furthermore, they get consumed with the need to improve everything in their life, sometimes including people as well. While there are many benefits to this personality type, there are also several challenges that arise when interacting with a One. Guilt, anger, depression, and emotional detachment can often hide the fact that Ones are loving, warm and sensitive souls beneath their perfection-seeking exteriors.

The One in action

Henry has been promoted to department head in his company, making him one of the new bosses for the employees at Café Fresh. Dana and Jane have worked side-by-side as assistant managers at the café for the past four years. They don't interact with higher-ups too often, so they were both initially indifferent when they found out that Henry would be joining the team.

Henry, however, is not like previous bosses. As a One, his approach is very hands-on. He immediately showed an interest in improving the department in every way, including productivity and worker conditions. He met with the supervisors, managers, and baristas at Café Fresh three times in his first week – sometimes sharing new policies that would be implemented and, other times, walking up and down the café while silently scanning for potential areas of improvement.

On one of their lunch breaks, Dana and Jane are surprised to find they have very different views of Henry. Jane has welcomed him with open arms. She is motivated by the enthusiastic vision he brings and admires his self-confidence. Dana chuckles as Jane uses the word "self-confident" and thinks "dominating" is a more appropriate word to describe Henry. She gets more and more fed-up each time Henry starts talking about a new idea.

In the weeks that follow, there is an unhealthy tension in the air that undermines Henry's goal of overall improvement. He senses this and gets disheartened. He thought the team would be excited about the prospect of improving their café and wonders why they seem resistant to progress.

One of the problems here is that Henry does not show respect for Dana's abilities. Having been in her position for several years, Dana feels that she knows what she is doing and doesn't need a new person to tell her how to do her job. Henry, however, has his own vision for what the perfect café looks like. His belief in his own vision is so strong that he forgets to consider whether the rest of the team, including Dana, is in agreement.

Furthermore, Dana feels that Henry's approach questions her abilities, which adds to her stress and frustration. Henry may believe Dana is exceptional at her job — perhaps that is even why he entrusts her with so many important changes. But as a One, Henry's focus is not on what Dana is already doing right, it is on what she could be doing better.

The simple fact is that both Henry and Dana are headstrong perfectionists. This means that they value autonomy in their jobs and have a hard time taking orders from anyone else. Dana may have reacted more positively if Henry clearly explained the vision he was chasing and gave the Café Fresh employees time to buy into the vision and brainstorm their own additions.

You might be wondering: is it possible that this is just a problem with Dana? Some employees wouldn't mind Henry's approach at all. In fact, Jane seemed perfectly happy. Why could that be?

Jane appreciates that Henry shows the tendency to have both a vision of the future and the ability to achieve it. As a Six, she will gladly follow someone with integrity and ability – qualities Ones have in abundance. Therefore, Henry's strong approach is just the thing to inspire the die-hard loyalty that Jane is eager to provide.

Personality profile of the One

Ones are renowned for being reliable and ambitious. Their pursuit for perfection means that they won't rest until the job is, not only done, but done correctly. Subsequently, people can rest assured that any project left in the hands of a One will be done on time and to the highest of standards. They may be the types of people who constantly seek improvement. Rather than seeing the glass as half empty or half full, they want to know why the glass can't be filled all the way. Not willing to settle for how things are, they search for ways to improve on things that other people are perfectly content with accepting. The downside to this, however, is that Ones can tend to be workaholics. Since perfection is rarely achieved, their pursuit for it will consume most of their time, leaving little for relaxation, recreation, and even relationships.

Some Ones believe that if something can be improved, it should be. Therefore, their minds tend to analyze everything — constantly looking for those finishing touches that will turn mediocre into a masterpiece. Other Ones latch onto a particular cause that needs reform. For example, a One might gravitate towards the fight to end social injustices or fervently demand environmental sustainability. However, those Ones may overlook some imperfections in their home when they return from work. Whether or not the One takes action on improving the faults they encounter, the core remains that they, more than anyone else, can identify what is right and wrong. Whether others agree with their beliefs on right and wrong, however, is another story entirely.

Ones are part of the gut center. For them, this manifests as an instinctual feeling of what is right and what is wrong. Henry knew what the 'right' café looked like and could spot deviations from his vision the moment he saw them. Even if he does not know exactly why something is right or wrong, he has a gut feeling that he strongly believes in. Some Ones are perfectly happy to base their actions and decisions on their gut feelings. Others will feel the need to rationalize their feelings with logic and consider all possible outcomes of acting on their instincts. In these cases, the One might spend so much time thinking about their beliefs, actions, and decisions that they mistake themselves for a person who is primarily motivated by reason and logic. The One's driving force, however, is instinct – after that, a logical explanation for that instinct may or may not follow.

Enneatypes in the gut center are most associated with the feeling of anger. For the One, anger might start to arise 1) when others do not understand that something is right or wrong or 2) when others (or themselves) fail to do the right thing. Since their minds are tuned to identify areas they can reform, Ones will find faults more often than not. Rather than accepting imperfection and moving on, a One will not only search for a solution, but will wonder why people have allowed such faults to exist in the first place. Ones may find that they are short tempered when things do not meet their standards. This anger is usually not aimed at other people involved, but rather at the situation itself. Unfortunately, most people won't understand this and will feel as though the One is angry with them personally. The One's search for perfection is not simply for the sake of perfection itself; rather it is to improve the world and the lives of those in it. Often others do not understand or appreciate this, as they find it hard to see that the One is actually a very emotional and compassionate person, even if their exterior seems harsh and serious.

Perhaps you know a One who does not seem short-tempered at all. This is possible because Ones often try to repress the emotion of anger in an attempt to be their own ideal of perfection. Alternatively, anger may be directed internally, which is one reason that Ones are an Enneatype prone to depression. When you consider that depression is also known as "anger directed inward," it begins to make sense why a One's anger might manifest in this way.

While Ones may seem harsh, critical, and/or emotionless, the fact is that they are very warm and caring individuals. They may hold you to the highest of standards, but the truth is that they hold themselves to even higher standards. Any criticism from a One should be taken as a challenge to become your best, not an attack on your character. Additionally, any emotional detachment from a One should not be taken at face value. Ones are very emotional, despite what their appearance might suggest. They simply allow logic to dominate their minds as they search for ways to justify their instinct, which can leave emotions ignored or set aside to be dealt with another time.

If you are a One, you are able to look at a situation and not only see what sits right in front of you, but also what could ideally be sitting right in front of you. You share an Enneatype with several people who have used their power for spreading immense amounts of good, such as Joan of Arc, Nelson Mandela, and Plato. Despite the stereotypes, you are not destined to always be critical and controlling. You may be able to spot flaws a mile away, but you can also spot opportunity. You recognize that regardless of how things are now, they can always get better.

Part V:
Going Deeper

Chapter 11: Growth and Stress Arrows

One common question in Enneagram workshops is: "Are we only one personality type?" The response to the question is both "yes and no!" The Enneagram is a dynamic system; we regularly move around to other Enneagram points depending on our needs and circumstances, so we are not restricted to only one point on the diagram. We invest time visiting and inhabiting other personality types while keeping our core personality type as our "home base." However, it is not a random course. The patterns or pathways that every personality type tends to pursue is demonstrated by the Enneagram diagram itself.

The lines of the Enneagram represent the paths we travel on when we experience shifts of awareness and behavior in our day-to-day lives. These lines are a critical component of the Enneagram and understanding them gives a more complete picture of any individual person. Each personality type is connected to two different types by arrows. In the Enneagram, these arrows depict the direction of movement a person is likely to take when they are unbalanced and unhealthy (stress arrow; direction of disintegration) and the direction a person will likely go in when they are improving as a person (growth arrow; direction of integration).

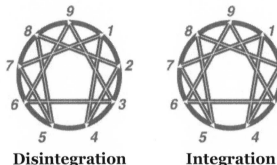

Disintegration   **Integration**

Having separate Enneagrams for the Direction of Integration and the Direction of Disintegration is not important. By removing the arrows and connecting the proper points with plain lines, both directions can be shown on one Enneagram.

We can move along the Enneagram lines, dipping from one point to the next. Sometimes we barely notice the change in our outlook because we go back and forth very quickly. Having said that, we may sometimes go through a more dramatic shift, or spend a considerable amount of time in a point that is not our basic personality type.

In the diagram itself, it appears that there is some inborn, organizing intelligence. This is how the Enneagram differs from other personality systems. The Enneagram is a holistic system based on symmetry and mathematics. The lines illustrate the way energy moves in repeated patterns and convey consequential information about our psychological patterns.

Some of the concepts underlying the "Lines of the Enneagram" theory are examined in the next segment. It's not strictly required to know this to understand personality types. If you prefer, you can skip over this section and go straight to the segment on "The Lines Interpreted for Each Personality Type" to see how the lines and growth arrows apply to your personality type.

The Theory Behind the Lines

If you take a look at the Enneagram, you will notice two overlapping sets of lines. One is the triangle joining focus points 3, 6, and 9. This "inner triangle" is an illustration of the "Law of Three" which comes up in both religious and secular contexts as indicated by tradition. This corresponds to the Holy Trinity, the three main aspects of Divinity – Father, Son, and Holy Ghost in Christian terms. Note that a Hindu Trinity also exists. In secular terms, The Law of Three may be described as thesis, antithesis, and synthesis.

George Gurdjieff brought the Enneagram to the West in 1915 and presented the concept in this way: the place initiating energy is point three (Holy Affirming); the place of energy development and resistance is point six (Holy Denying); while the place of energy meditation and harmonization is point nine (Holy Reconciling). The interesting thing about this is that the personality types whom we associate with these points appear to embody some of these characteristics. Threes possess that wonderful initiating, go-forward spirit. Sixes regularly say "Hang on a minute: how about we develop this idea further, let's find what's not right with it and think of a better plan." People who seek balance and harmony are Nines, as they are innate mediators. In a more humorous vein, we sometimes make descriptions of personality types 3, 6, and 9 as exhibiting the qualities of Holy Yes, Holy No, and Holy Maybe.

These three personality types are connected by the lines of this inner triangle. We will examine how they move back and forth from one point to another under various conditions in the next segment. In any occasion, there is something extremely valuable about this idea of "three-ness." We need to have enough motivation and "initiating" energy to begin a novel project or activity. But as we are all aware, things don't just move forward in a straight line. This certainly is evident in our work on personal growth.

Often times, there is resistance or some kind of impediment in our way – either something in ourselves or something in our environment which we need to overcome (frequently both). If we are able to engage this set of impediments in an intelligent manner and consider it as a helpful part of the procedure, our original plan or intention develops into something much more successful. If we are able to have a decent discussion, or a gainful conflict between the initiating parts and the resisting parts, we can move to some sort of resolution or synthesis. Without this procedure, however, projects or people don't develop and grow into something more prominent.

The lines that associate points 1, 4, 2, 8, 5, and 7 is the second arrangement of lines inside the Enneagram. This is used to illustrate the "Law of Seven," a number set which is associated with the seven notes of our musical scale. The Law of Seven has to do with the movement of energy – the progression of steps or the chain of occasions in each activity or project, while the Law of Three has to do with qualities of energy or three various kinds of force at work. The Law of Seven has been found very helpful by some people in planning their work, making sure to incorporate the important steps and the interventions that are key components of keeping things moving toward a successful end; however, this is outside the scope of our present discussion. For the time being, we can simply notice how this set of lines, and the connections between the numbers on this arrangement of lines, inform us about personality types.

If the number 1 is divided by the number 7, we get a repeating decimal: .142857142... So the lines inside the Enneagram follow this progression of numbers. The personality types here (Types 1, 4, 2, 8, 5, and 7) move back and forth along these lines under various internal conditions according to Enneagram theory.

Directions of Disintegration (Stress)

The sequence of numbers 1-4-2-8-5-7-1 shows the Direction of Disintegration or Stress for every type. This implies that, an average to unhealthy One undergoing stress will ultimately have habits of an average to unhealthy Four; the stress of an average to unhealthy Four will be similar to an average to unhealthy Two; the stress mode of an average to unhealthy Two will be similar to that of an Eight, an Eight will act out like a Five under stress, a Five under stress will act out like a Seven, and a Seven under stress will act out like a One. (Awareness is one easy way to recall the sequence, that 1-4 or 14 doubles to 28, and that doubles to 57—or almost so.

Thus, 1-4-2-8-5-7—and the sequence starts again as it returns to 1.) Likewise, the sequence is 9-6-3-9 on the equilateral triangle: a Nine will act out like a Six when stressed out, a Six will act out like a Three when stressed out, and a Three, when stressed out, will act out like a Nine. (This sequence can be remembered if you think of the numerical values diminishing as the types become more stressed and reactive). If the arrows' direction on the Enneagram below is to be followed, you will see how this works.

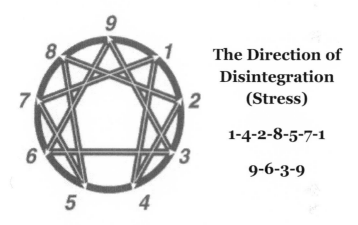

The Direction of Disintegration (Stress)

1-4-2-8-5-7-1

9-6-3-9

Directions of Integration (Growth)

For each type, The Direction of Integration or Growth is demonstrated by the reverse of the sequences for disintegration. Each type advances toward integration in a path that is the opposite of its unhealthy course. Therefore, the sequence for the Direction of Integration is 1-7-5-8-2-4-1: an integrating One will go to Seven, an integrating Seven will go to Five, an integrating Five will go to Eight, an integrating Eight will go to Two, an integrating Two will go to Four, and an integrating Four will go to One. The sequence On the equilateral triangle is 9-3-6-9: an integrating Nine goes to Three, an integrating Three goes to Six, and an integrating Six goes to Nine. You can see how this functions by following the direction of the arrows on the Enneagram below:

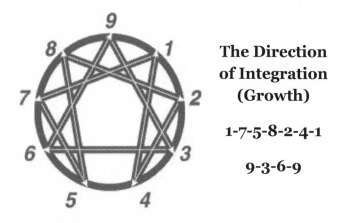

The Direction of Integration (Growth)

1-7-5-8-2-4-1

9-3-6-9

Regardless of your personality type, the types in both your Integration or Growth Direction and your Disintegration or Stress Direction are pertinent influences. You must consider the basic type and wing as well as the two types in the Directions of Integration and Disintegration to acquire a complete picture of yourself (or of another person). The factors denoted by those four types blend into your total personality and give the framework for understanding what influences you. For example, it is rare to exclusively have a type Two personality. A Two usually possesses either a One-wing or a Three-wing, and the overall personality of the Two is influenced by its Direction of Disintegration (Eight) and its Direction of Integration (Four).

The Arrows Interpreted for each Enneagram Type

Type One Direction of Integration: Seven
Type One Direction of Disintegration: Four

Ones seek perfection, which can sometimes be pursued by following orderly and rational procedures. Ones, however, can sometimes become overly rigid and methodical to ensure they do things the exact right way. Healthy Ones relax strict and rigid pursuits of perfection and integrate toward the Type Seven to incorporate spontaneity and joy into their lives. They still hold onto their strong convictions and integrity, but balance that with the joy that is necessary for fulfillment. When Ones are not able to feel at ease with imperfections in themselves and the world at large, their dissatisfaction can grow so intense that they become hypercritical, moody, and depressed, like an unhealthy Four.

<u>Type Two Direction of Integration:</u> Four
<u>Type Two Direction of Disintegration:</u> Eight

Twos are "people pleasers" and are naturally hospitable and friendly. When they are trying to make others happy, they may seek approval to validate themselves. Happy, healthy Twos are able to use their natural hospitality to integrate the sincerity and awareness of Type Fours. They are still looking to put others first and to be their usual, hospitable selves, but are more focused on the sincere act of serving rather than seeking approval. When they are uncomfortable with the reaction from others, such as feeling unloved or unappreciated, they can take on the domineering or coercive behaviors of an unhealthy Type Eight.

<u>Type Three Direction of Integration:</u> Six
<u>Type Three Direction of Disintegration:</u> Nine

Threes are charming and ambitious. They earn the title of "achievers" when they are working hard to make good things happen for themselves. This can make them competitive and work-focused in their fight to get ahead. At their best, Threes look out for their own best interests as well as the interests of others like healthy, open-hearted Sixes. When they are distressed, Threes tend to become the opposite of their usually engaged and energetic selves and become apathetic and slow to take action like the unhealthy, slothful traits of Nines.

Type Four Direction of Integration: One
Type Four Direction of Disintegration: Two

Fours are highly individualistic and want to express their true selves above all else. Their desire to follow their hearts can make them prone to mood swings and self-indulgent behavior, but it also fuels their profoundly creative minds. When they are healthy and focused, Fours can become diligent, detail-oriented workers like a Type One. When they feel censored or inauthentic, they can become clingy or critical like an unhealthy Two.

Type Five Direction of Integration: Eight
Type Five Direction of Disintegration: Seven

Fives are investigators who want to learn all about the world, but from a distance. They sometimes struggle to get involved with what's happening around them, but when they do, they are all in. When they feel comfortable and confident, healthy Fives show more traits of a healthy Eight and use their knowledge to be more decisive and involved. When they are stressed, they retreat into their own thoughts and projects and become more avoidant of whatever is making them uncomfortable – much like an unhealthy Seven would.

Type Six Direction of Integration: Nine
Type Six Direction of Disintegration: Three

Sixes seek security and are always looking for reassurance. They have a natural tendency to look for problems and spot potential issues a mile away, making them prepared, reliable people. When they are comfortable, Sixes take on the healthy traits of an easy-going Nine. They are more able to relax and "go with the flow." When they reach unmanageable levels of anxiety, Sixes take on the more selfish, competitive traits of a Three.

Type Seven Direction of Integration: Five
Type Seven Direction of Disintegration: One

Sevens are the fun-loving, active types on the Enneagram. They like to chase experiences and run from boredom and discomfort. This trait can make them seem distracted, but when they are healthy, Sevens take on the more focused, goal-oriented traits of a Five. When they are experiencing stress that threatens their fun, excitement, or freedom, Sevens become critical toward themselves and others, bringing out the unhealthy traits of a One.

Type Eight Direction of Integration: Two
Type Eight Direction of Disintegration: Five

Eights are all-action. They know what they want and will do what it takes to get it. Their main motivation is to be in control and independent, which can make them confrontational. At their best, Eights not only want what's best for them, but also want what's best for others – like a healthy Two does. When they are experiencing stress, Eights become possessive of their resources such as time and energy – like an unhealthy Five.

Type Nine Direction of Integration: Three
Type Nine Direction of Disintegration: Six

Nines are easy-going types who want to avoid conflict. Their desire to keep the peace make them come off as very agreeable, but often costs them their own wants and needs. They avoid "rocking the boat" by being slow to act, but this keeps them from their fullest potential. When they are healthy, Nines are more active and ambitious like a Type Three. However, when they must face conflict or learn to handle confrontation, Nines take on the more anxious, nervous traits of a Six.

The ultimate goal is for every one of us to "move around" the Enneagram, integrating what each type stands for and acquiring the healthy benefits of each type. The idea is to end up a balanced, fully-functioning individual who can take advantage of the potential and possibilities embedded in each type. Every one of the types of the Enneagram stands for various vital aspects of what we need to accomplish. The personality type we start life with is ultimately less vital than how well we utilize our type as the starting point for our self-development and self-realization.

Chapter 12: Personality Wings

The Enneagram is strategically arranged such that the characteristics of one personality type blend into the characteristics of the types on either side of it. For example, a Six is likely to have more in common with a Five or Seven (its neighbors), as compared to an Eight or a Nine.

This goes back to a point that we mentioned earlier: no one is purely one singular personality type. Everyone will have a little bit of each of the nine types within them, but one of those types will be dominant – and one of the dominant type's neighbors will influence the way the dominant type is expressed. The neighbor that more strongly influences the dominant type is called the "wing."

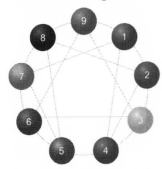

In the basic wing hypothesis, Ones can have a 9 or 2 as their wing. That means, if you are a One, you might be a One wing Two (1w2) or a One wing Nine (1w9). In this case, you can best understand the whole of your personality by putting the characteristics of the One into consideration as they uniquely mix with the characteristics of either the 9 or the 2, depending on which is your particular wing.

Twos can have a 1 or 3 as their wing; Threes can have a 2 or 4 as their wing; Fours can have a 3 or 5 as their wing; Fives can have a 4 or 6 as their wing; Sixes can have a 5 or 7 as their wings; Sevens can have a 6 or 8 as their wing; Eights can have a 7 or 9 as their wing; and Nines can have an 8 or 1 as their wing.

Any type's potential wings can be seen on the Enneagram symbol by noting the numbers that fall on either side of that personality type on the diagram. Wings do not change a person's character structure and core motivations. However, they explain some of the differences we see in the behaviors of people who share an Enneatype.

Your general personality is dominated by your basic type, but we can think of the wing as the "second side" of your personality. Personality wings must be taken into consideration if we want to fully utilize the Enneagram to better understand others and even ourselves. The wing may sometimes supplement a person's dominant personality, but other times may add seemingly contradictory (yet important) components that give nuance to a person's motivations and behaviors.

In our experience, we haven't seen many people who appear to have two wings, but it is possible that a person may be equally influenced by both of their type's Enneagram neighbors. If you are an Eight, for example, this would mean that your personality is equal parts 7 and 9. This has been debated among the different traditions of the Enneagram. Some educators believe that a person possesses just a single wing, while some educators say there are no wings at all; nonetheless, individuals can possess a single wing, double wings, or none at all.

Everyone has two wings by the strictest definition. In your personality, both types adjacent to your basic type operate, since every individual possesses the elements of *all* of the nine types. Having said that, when we discuss "having two wings" we aren't referring to the fundamental principle that all Enneatypes are present in an individual, instead, we are referring to the less common occurrence where two types "tie" for the role of second-place in the degree to which they influence the dominant type. From our observations, we can conclude that there is a single dominant wing in most individuals, but that the two-wing hypothesis may apply to some.

In most people, the dominant wing is unquestionably more essential, though the supposed second wing is always working to a certain extent. For instance, Twos with Three-wings are quite distinguishable from Twos with One-wings, and while Twos with Three-wings have a One-wing, it is more negligible than the Three-wing. Therefore, it is clearer to refer to a type's "wing" instead of its "dominant wing," and this essentially means the same thing. [Note: Many people notice their so-called "second wing" improves in the latter half of their lives.]

Of course, before you can evaluate which wing you have, you must recognize your core type. To comprehend the impact of your wing, the ideal approach is to read personality profiles with the full description of your type and its possible wings. Likewise, you should read descriptions of the two types adjacent to your basic type and reflect on which applies best to you. We have already discussed profiles for each of the core types and we will delve deeper into descriptions of each wing shortly.

The wing or wings of a person should be understood because it helps people understand, for example, why unexpected behavior is seen in a Five wing Six in comparison to a Five wing Four. Because a Five wing Six has twofold mental energy (both Sixes and Fives are head center types), they will generally be more cerebral and careful than a Five wing Four. Since Fours are in the heart center, Fives with Four-wings will generally be more enthusiastic, with what can be called a double sense of abandonment. Both Fours and Fives have a shared sense of existential abandonment, but they display this sense in different ways. Fours realize they have been abandoned by people and cry about it in a phenomenon called "wet abandonment." On the other hand, Fives have figured out how to live in this state and never cry again, and the phenomenon is therefore called "dry" abandonment.

The careful arrangement of each personality

type on the Enneagram gives rise to wings that can be used as an extra tool to guide our self-comprehension and self-development. Since both wings are accessible by us all, we identify whether our balance is tipped toward either wing and then work to become more balanced. When we identify and integrate positive qualities of both wings, we gain immense possibilities for growth and development.

The following is basic information on wings for each core Enneagram type and how these wings supplement the core type.

Type 1 wing 9 (1w9)

If you are a 1w9, you likely find it easy to unwind and relax and you don't have to put much effort into it. When conflicts arise, you are cool and calm about them and consider the opinions of other people, especially the people whom you respect.

You are an idealist. You are ethical, critical, and focused.

You see all sides of the coin and you are very collaborative. You tend to go with the flow. You let events unfold naturally, which makes it easier for you to relax and allows you to trust others.

Because of your Nine wing, you tend to procrastinate on difficult yet important tasks at times. Other times, you neglect yourself in order to get things done.

Type 1 wing 2 (1w2)

If you are a 1w2, you are very generous, people-focused, warm, and full of compassion.

You have the qualities of activists and advocates.

You are very demanding, but also caring and thoughtful.

You are typically great at understanding others. You may even be an empath. However, you realize that you can't always save the world, so you try to improve yourself as often as you try to improve situations and people. You are very optimistic that change is possible.

You tend to put others before you, even if it means you must neglect your own needs. This means you often end up feeling that you are being exploited or victimized. You live for appreciation and you are very sensitive. Therefore, to feel accepted and worthwhile, you spend time doing what you believe will improve the world.

Type 2 wing 1 (2w1)

If you are a 2w1, you pay attention to detail and are great at reading people and situations. You know how to stand up for yourself, are firm when you need to be, and are able to say "no" when someone crosses the line.

At the same time, you are an altruist. You are warm, enjoy serving others, and are a people-pleaser.

You hate bending the rules and never break them. You have high moral values, which drives you to help anyone who is in need. You understand your limits and you are honest to yourself.

You may be led to neglect yourself as you pursue higher desires and unrealistic ideals. If lofty expectations are not met, you feel stressed and hurt, which may result in resentment and self-criticism. Also, your concern and pursuit of justice for the underdog leads to a risk of overworking and burnout.

Type 2 wing 3 (2w3)

If you are a 2w3, you regularly seek being noticed and are happy to acknowledge that you have a deep desire to be successful.

You are a giver. You are adaptable, supportive, and friendly.

You have the ability to coexist with people and

to adapt to other people in a wide variety of diverse settings. You are organized, focused, and a selfless team player who keeps the best interests of the entire team in mind.

You are somewhat detached from your inner self and needs. Instead, you are more involved with the pursuit of success – which means you may be a workaholic. You work and help others to be recognized by important and influential individuals.

Type 3 wing 2 (3w2)

If you are a 3w2, you are generous with your time and resources and are sensitive to other peoples' feelings. You often focus on helping others in your personal and professional life.

You are a motivator. You are charming, narcissistic, ambitious, and encouraging.

You balance the Three's task-oriented behavior with the Two's fondness for people. You value people as contributors to your success as much as you value them as individuals.

You are outward-focused and seek approval. Your Two wing amplifies this need to please key stakeholders. As you adapt to what other people want, you run the risk of burning out. You may become overly concerned with other peoples' expectations instead of being true to yourself, which means you may end up disappointed if your achievements are not acknowledged.

Type 3 wing 4 (3w4)

If you are a 3w4, you are in touch with your feelings, likely enjoy artistic expression, and/or have high levels of artistic appreciation. You like to take part in emotional discussions and have a deep personal presence.

You are an achiever. You are creative, ambitious, and image-conscious.

You value the adventure of self-development. You can become true to yourself when you tune into your inner voice. You see relationships as a form of mutual exchange and don't just engage with people when you need something, which means you are able to bring sensitivity and insight to the table when you engage with others.

Your Four-wing brings introversion and distance to your personality. While you value being successful, you may always have a sense that there is something missing, and you may jump into brief and intense relationships to try and fill that void.

Type 4 wing 3 (4w3)

If you are a 4w3, you have the energy to get things done. You are self-confident. You prefer staying on the front lines and getting noticed.

You are introspective, original, moody, and unique.

You have a strong desire to be influential in the outside world; therefore, you express yourself and engage people, especially via creative fantasies.

You are a very genuine person and try to always express yourself authentically. You have a very strong desire to look good and impress other people.

To get away from moments of inner unrest, you

may perform an act instead of actually producing and engaging. In times like these, you may lack substance – leading to a dramatic and flamboyant act rather than real self-expression.

Rather than fixing yourself, you may try to fix the world around you when things get particularly stressful.

Type 4 wing 5 (4w5)

If you are a 4w5, you are analytical and objective. You have the ability to consider situations from all angles and keep a calm demeanor during your assessment. You regularly show self-restraint and self-containment.

You are an artist. You are unconventional, self-conscious, and depressive.

Your intuition and subjective impressions are perfectly in balance with logic, reason, and objective observation. You perceive the world objectively and don't take much personally. This brings about a balance of attachment and detachment, as well as emotional control, and you tend to become more restrained and less impulsive as you think and connect with your feelings.

You have a tendency to over-rationalize. You often feel alienated and marginalized. On top of that, you struggle when trying to bond with other people. This is partially because you are a very private person and isolate yourself, especially when you are going through a rough time.

Type 5 wing 4 (5w4)

If you are a 5w4, you are expressive, emotionally sensitive, have aesthetic insight, appreciate the arts, and may even be an artist yourself.

You are a true visionary. You are provocative, cerebral, and creative.

You easily connect intuition and analytical ability, which is your right and left brain. When your thoughts and feelings are connected, your energy and expression are in harmony.

Your Four wing means you bring passion to your relationships and can connect affectionately and intimately. Even still, you are unique and are often misunderstood. This can cause you to become depressed and moody.

Type 5 wing 6 (5w6)

If you are a 5w6, you are a team player, place value on loyalty, and possess enhanced intuitive insight. You know how to put your facts together and thoroughly analyze the external environment.

You are an excellent observer. You are perfectionistic, investigative, socially awkward, and contrarian.

You look at evidence rationally before taking and defending a position or perspective. You place a lot of faith in yourself as well as others, leading to a commitment to individuals and causes. You can connect profoundly with teams and groups, but when you start to mistrust people, you become suspicious and withdraw.

Type 6 wing 5 (6w5)

If you are a 6w5, you are internally focused and

self-contained, therefore knowing when it is or is not appropriate to be reactive. Additionally, you have a passion for scholarship and are on an unending quest for knowledge.

You are a guardian. You are dependable, investigative, cynical, and contrarian.

Instead of seeking validation, you trust and rely on your inner self. This gives you more confidence to make sound judgments based on your own rationality and experiences. You tend to analyze the situation which helps you to put your own fears in perspective, makes you open to other perspectives, and assists you in making sensible decisions.

The Six's tendency towards fear and anxiety is amplified by the Five-wing. Instead of confronting issues head-on, you tend to back away from confrontation. In difficult situations, you try to remove and detach yourself from the problem. In order to feel safe, you often turn to dogma or inflexible systems.

Type 6 wing 7 (6w7)

Sixes often see the glass as half empty, while Sevens often see it as half full. If you are a 6w7, you see the entire glass and therefore have the tendency to be highly energetic, cheerful, optimistic, and relaxed.

You are loyal, reliable, wary, entertaining, and balanced.

You don't automatically imagine the worst because you are usually quite optimistic and trusting in the goodness of other people. You are jolly, playful and light-hearted. You are an extrovert and have the ability to see different perspectives, which gives you an innovative side.

You hate conflict and often find a way to escape from it when it arises. Your worst fear is that you will suffer from pain and thus, you try to avoid this by distracting yourself, often with insignificant things.

Type 7 wing 6 (7w6)

If you are a 7w6, you have the ability to comprehend situations as being both half-empty and half-full. Your Six wing gives you a high sense of perception and ability to anticipate possible problems, which makes you more intentional and less impulsive than the core Seven.

You are an enthusiast. You are gregarious, spontaneous, impulsive, and quick-acting.

You are committed to your goals and you investigate things in depth. You long for freedom without any inhibition. You are a realist and you tend to stay fully present in the moment, which allows you to be highly productive.

Planning is a challenging task for you because of deeply rooted self-doubt. You tend to be flighty, which exacerbates underlying fears. When you are not responsible, you often feel a deep sense of guilt.

Type 7 wing 8 (7w8)

If you are a 7w8, you are straightforward, assertive, and powerful. You have what it takes to turn ideas into action and you have a grounded presence.

You are an excitement seeker. You are impatient, escapist, extroverted, and engaging.

You are self-driven and know how to execute your plans. You are usually very honest in self-disclosure and interactions with other people, which is a primary reason that you are perceived as being very grounded.

You sometimes force your ideas onto other people. Your assertiveness may turn into aggressiveness. You may act superior to others and end up seeming self-absorbed. Your desire for more and the desire for prompt satisfaction can lead to you exploiting other people for your own personal gains.

Type 8 wing 7 (8w7)

If you are an 8w7, you are independent, high-spirited, and adventurous. You love to try new things and love to experiment in both your professional and your personal lives.

You are a rebel. You are fierce, power-seeking, and defiant. However, your Seven-wing adds a light-heartedness to the typically more serious

Eight outlook on life.

You balance the urgency to act with perspective and planning. You connect with other individuals and exchange ideas instead of "doing it alone," and you are great at communicating your ideas with others.

When you experience intense passion, you become desperate to satisfy your wants and desires. Additionally, the influence of your Seven wing makes you prone to addictive tendencies.

Type 8 wing 9 (8w9)

If you are an 8w9, you are warmer, less reactive, and calmer than the core Eight. You solicit and pay attention to other people's opinions because you tend to be group-oriented.

You have a boss mentality. You are a leader, but can also be bullying and challenging.

The impulsiveness of your core type is balanced with the Nine's laid-back approach, making you calm and receptive to others. You have a strong will to let events unfold and happen naturally rather than forcing situations to go your way. Your strong sense of autonomy is balanced by a sense of unity.

Because of your Nine wing, you may hyper-focus on work so much that you begin to neglect yourself.

Type 9 wing 8 (9w8)

If you are a 9w8, you display solidity and forcefulness while still listening to other people's opinions. Your Eight wing gives you a "take-charge" attitude, helps you assert your point-of-view more readily, and assists you in making quick and clear decisions.

You are a mediator. You are conversational, optimistic, and inspiring.

Your Eight-wing welcomes you to get in touch with your autonomy, authority, and power. You balance the drive to merge with other people with a sense of uniqueness and individuality, which makes you more influential and confident. When you speak up, your Eight's boldness subdues your Nine's fear of attack.

You may sometimes communicate aggressively when you feel resistant or rebellious, which may lead to issues with authority. Additionally, you may become overly focused on the quest for superficial pleasures, rather than focusing on the needs of your real self and genuine desires.

Type 9 wing 1 (9w1)

If you are a 9w1, you are attentive to details, precise, and punctual. Your One-wing increases your overall focus, clarity, judgment, and insight.

You are a peacemaker. You are independent, stubborn, and philosophical.

You have a balance of easy-going Nineness and the more principled and structured Oneness. Rather than quietly accepting the problems that arise in your life, you demonstrate a willingness to work on righting what is wrong. You move into action with certainty and purpose.

You may not be expressive of your needs and disappointments due to a fear of alienating other people. Additionally, you may get caught up in what you "should" do rather than what you want to do. You are always trying to move yourself and the world around you towards perfection, but since you often have a fear of being wrong, this ambition could be hampered by distractions and procrastination.

Chapter 13: Instinctual Variants and Subtypes

Over time, humans have evolved to have three basic survival strategies, also called basic instincts. Every individual operates according to one of these three instinctual Enneagram variants (also called subtypes) in addition to the Enneagram type:

- The self-preservation instinct (managing oneself, reacting to perceived threats and needs)
- The sexual or one-to-one (dealing with someone else, coupling or primary relationships)
- The social instinct (creation of social structures within communities, dealing with a group)

Just as a person's wing colors the way they express their core Enneagram type, a person's instinctual variant will add another dimension to their core motivations and behaviors.

In everyday life, our subtype pattern is one of the primary ways that we "fall asleep." This means that we often don't notice the effect our subtype has on us as clearly as other people notice it in us. Others are most attuned to these effects when they themselves have a different subtype. This can lead to difficulties if a person only notices the actions you take as a result of your instinctual variant, but cannot comprehend the exact reason why you are taking those actions. Without deliberate communication over time, even small differences in subtypes can erode a relationship if either party cannot comprehend the motivations behind the other's actions. Therefore, to live healthier and more balanced lives, it is helpful to know our instinctual patterns and how those patterns influence our day-to-day. When we have a thorough understanding of ourselves, we can more accurately communicate our needs and desires to the people in our lives. Understanding instinctual variants also gives us another tool to understand the view points of others and prevent misunderstandings and conflicts.

The Self-Preservation Variant

Individuals of the self-preservation variant generally try to be independent and comfortable. They pay careful attention to their health, house, and financial position because their well-being is vital to them. They have less interest in interpersonal contact, are normally less spontaneous, and don't exhibit as much emotion as individuals of the other two subtypes.

Since this variant is primarily concerned with comfort, physical safety, and well being, their priorities revolve around securing a comfortable and orderly way of life in regard to food, housing, money, clothing, and physical health. They may easily stress about issues such as money, food, how they will obtain these resources, when they will obtain it, if they will be able to adequately use it, etc.

They will also place large value in security and being in an overall comfortable environment (temperature, lighting, food quality, comfortable furniture, aesthetics). They tend to have a good sense of finances and are able to create a secure environment in the workplace and home by acquiring skills to ensure the orderly flow of life.

If people of this variant do not get what they want, they may resort to excessive comforting activities such as overbuying, overeating, over-purging, over-stocking, oversleeping, under-sleeping, overindulging in aesthetics or comfort foods.

The Sexual Variant

Individuals of the sexual variant are especially interested in one-to-one contact. They seek intimacy and, though not necessarily, this may show in their sexuality. It is very important for them to be in a relationship. As they have more energy and are more temperamental, they are the most passionate of the subtypes. They care less about duty and rules and have no problem with being involved in fights.

The sexual variant is primarily concerned with intense experiences, contacts, and connections. They are highly exploratory and their end goal is to discover something to "complete" them internally (deep discussions, ski jumps, exciting movies, etc). They are usually stressed by the absence of an intense experience or connection, as well as the absence of intense emotional or mental stimulation.

While their primary focus is on individuals and attractions, they can give off sensuality and intense energy. They constantly look outside of themselves for the individual or situation that will complete them.

When they don't get what they want, they cope with it in one of two ways, depending on their secondary instincts. They may give scattered attention to people and things, lose focus, and become sexually promiscuous. On the other hand, they may run away from intense experiences and connections – showing a fearful and dysfunctional demeanor toward sex, intimacy, and other intense "completing" experiences.

The Social Variant

Individuals of the social variant prefer to be in teams or groups. Compared to the other subtypes, they are more interested in the position that they and other people have in a group and, consequently, are highly concerned with status. As they constantly want to be acknowledged, they try hard to fit in and be pleasant.

The social variant is primarily concerned with building a sense of individual value, accomplishment, and securing a place with other people via interaction in a broader sense (through the family, nation, world, community, group, subculture, mainstream culture). However, they are primarily stressed and concerned about their ability to adjust to other people and be acceptable, along with other people's reactions to them (e.g., whether they are being accepted or not). Because of this concern with what others think of them, people of the social variant may feel stressed by intimacy, so they often avoid it.

Their primary focus is the approval and status of their self and of other people in any number of various groups. They have a strong affinity for the "subtle" power structures and politics, knowing what is happening in the world, and a contextual intelligence that enables them to see both their efforts and their broader context in the world.

Their primary ambition is to interact with individuals in a way that will build their personal value, their sense of achievement, and their security of place with other people. They also love to touch base with other people to feel safe, alive, and energized, and this may involve the pursuit of attention, fame, success, honor, recognition, leadership, appreciation, and the security of being involved in something bigger than themselves.

When they don't get what they want, they may cope with it in an unhealthy manner by exhibiting poor social skills and antisocial behavior, along with hating and doubting the society at large. Their resentfulness is a result of having had to change to gain approval, and it may lead to avoiding social situations altogether and being against doing what is important to get along with others.

Primary, Secondary, and Neglected Instincts

When people discuss their instinctual variants, they will often use the abbreviations Sp (self-preserving), Sx (sexual), and So (social). You'll also notice that people generally report two variants – listing their dominant variant first and their secondary variant second. The third variant is sometimes called a "blind-spot" because it tends to be neglected due to an over-reliance on the first two instincts. In line with this idea of a being a "blind-spot," the tertiary instinct is usually left out when people list their instinctual variants. For example, a Type 5 person with a dominant self-preservation instinct and a secondary sexual instinct might identify as Enneagram Type 5 Sp/Sx. Even though this reporting structure leaves out an explicit mention of the person's blind spot, we can learn a lot about a person by considering how their blind spot will color the way they move through the world.

People who are Sx/So and So/Sx share a <u>self-preservation blind spot</u>. They are likely to disregard building a sense of personal value, achievement, and security. They may also lack awareness of their body's requirement for food and sleep, and may not prioritize the management of time and resources to establish a lifestyle that is orderly. Consequently, they may also have trouble amassing the money and resources required for security.

People who are Sp/So and So/Sp share a <u>sexual blind spot</u>. They are likely to have a dampened sense of the typical human longing to build personal value, achievement, and status in the opinion of others. They often neglect stimulating their mind and emotions in ways that elicit deep excitement, enthusiasm, intimate experiences, and unfamiliar experiences. They may fall into routines and, in spite of their existing social connections, may feel a strange disconnect from friends, spouses, and family.

People who are Sp/Sx and Sx/Sp share a <u>social blind spot</u>. They may be unaware of the human need to connect with the world in a broader sense. They do not chase the sense of security that comes from gathering in communities and do not have the typical desire for the approval of others. This can lead to frequent misunderstandings with allies, friends, supporters, and family members.

The 27 Subtypes

Having examined the three variants, let's look at the 27 subtypes:

* * *

Type 1 *with Self-preservation*: The Pioneer. Either extremely anxious or self-controlled, this subtype is concerned with security and survival; and secures material possessions to ensure they are always equipped to do the right thing. Self-preservation Ones try to subdue nature and impose order on the natural world by prioritizing their home, family, and resources such as food and money. Too much self-sacrifice, however, can lead to deep resentment and physical tension.

Type 1 *with Sexual*: The Evangelist. With clear standards and rules for appropriate behavior, the sexual One keeps a highly charged instinctual center under strict self-control, which may sometimes lead to overzealousness. To avoid self-recrimination, keeping a partner's attention is crucial to them. They may experience jealousy toward other people who appear to have more space for self-expression or even jealousy towards their partner.

<u>Type 1 *with Social*</u>: The Social Reformer. Comfortable with a secure social role and a clear set of rules, this subtype is typically friendly and gregarious on one's own turf. However, an emphasis on doing things the correct way can make it difficult to adjust to new situations, and can also create resentment or criticism toward other people who may be acting "incorrectly."

* * *

<u>Type 2 *with Self-preservation*</u>: The Nurturer. Excelling in creating personable, warm relationships with many different types of people, this subtype spends a lot of attention on nurturing and supporting others, which can lead to a feeling of entitlement in regards to getting one's own needs met. Their insistence on going last can lead to traits such as false modesty or a prideful attitude.

<u>Type 2 *with Sexual*</u>: The Lover. To win the approval of and make a connection with selected individuals in their relationships, this subtype utilizes all of the Two's ability for interpersonal

attunement. The utilization of body language and sensual tones can be seen as seductive, although not necessarily in a sexual way. Sexual Twos also sometimes appear aggressive and demand recognition or personal attention.

Type 2 _with Social_: The Ambassador. This subtype gains self-esteem through both visible achievements and social approval. They empathize and adjust to other people's demands to make sure they have an important or even indispensable role within an organization or group cause. For the ambassador, being allied with the appropriate people is usually more important than taking center stage.

* * *

Type 3 _with Self-preservation_: The Company Man/Woman. This subtype will do hard work, good performance, and maintain their public image for the sake of material success. The Self-preservation Three is often financially secure, with a decent home, as well as significant drive and energy. The danger is becoming overly identified with one's role at work, and therefore losing contact with one's real self.

<u>Type 3 _with Sexual_</u>: The Movie Star. This subtype strives to create a successful image centered on gender identity and issues. Their charisma or personal power rests on being attractive as a man or woman. However, under the surface, they may be confused about their real sexuality. Whether in personal relationships or on stage, the sexual Three tends to remain in the performer role.

<u>Type 3 _with Social_</u>: The Politician. The drive for success is directed toward knowing the right individuals, winning social approval, and accomplishing power in social institutions – whether in business, government, or groups. Through propaganda and image-making, there can either be genuine social leadership or simply self-aggrandizement.

* * *

<u>Type 4 _with Self-preservation_</u>: The Creative Individualist. In this subtype, there is a will to jump into situations that are new, to attempt risks, to keep pushing when the preservation instinct is activated, and to pack up and move in order to seek a better life. These actions may appear reckless to others, but it can work well

with an unorthodox, artistic, or creative style. This subtype feels pressure from the pull between wanting to acquire material security and feeling disconnected from it.

Type 4 *with Sexual*: The Dramatic. This subtype takes other people's strength or power as an individual challenge, and their own value tends to rise and fall based on comparison to others. This sense of constant competition helps to overcome feelings of inner inadequacy, and creates the motivation to formulate and refine a personal agenda.

Type 4 *with Social*: The Critical Commentator. Social situations can create feelings of inadequacy, with envy directed toward other individuals' status or appearance of belonging. This subtype tries to establish an acceptable social role, and can sometimes be the emotional truth-teller for the group. The Critical Commentator regularly feels a need to resolve the balance between individual authenticity and social expectations.

* * *

Type 5 *with Self-preservation:* The Castle Defender. The home can be referred to as one's castle, and a place to feel safe in and withdraw from the world. This subtype is concerned with having sufficient supplies, which can cause hoarding. Also, they may have no sense of allegiance to any geographical area, forever traveling or moving from one place to another.

Type 5 *with Sexual:* The Secret Agent. From the inner, private world in sexual relationships, this subtype will share deep confidences. The pressure between needing to preserve autonomy and needing to make contact can be reflected by a profound reserve or a secretive quality.

Type 5 *with Social:* The Professor. This subtype possesses a hunger for mastery and knowledge of society's sacred language and symbols. At the same time, this subtype can end up being an observer or teacher by over-emphasizing analysis and interpretation –limiting their relationships with other people.

* * *

Type 6 with *Self-preservation:* The Family Loyalist. This subtype has a fear of being neglected and left out in the cold, but beats fear by using their personal warmth to make connections and agreements with other people. There is a need to stay within well-known boundaries and an avoidance of taking risks. This is due to events in early life where there was an absence of warmth or a threat to security.

Type 6 *with Sexual*: The Warrior. The Warrior is dependent on overcoming or avoiding fear through willpower, bravery, and physical strength, or through the strength of intellect and ideological positions. Fear and self-doubt are dealt with by directing one's idealism and keen perceptiveness into creating beauty in the environment, which helps to create some control and stability.

Type 6 *with Social:* The Social Guardian. This subtype has an overwhelming need to be clear about their role in societal groups. To feel safe from rejection, Social Sixes must be certain of the rules and must be clear about agreements with friends and colleagues. In some cases, they may be ambivalent about belonging, and feel that carrying out one's duty can be both a burden and a calling.

* * *

<u>Type 7 _with Self-preservation_</u>: The Gourmand. This subtype likes to enjoy an abundant way of life within a circle of family and friends. The self-preservation Seven places emphasis on sharing great ideas and conversation, making elaborate meals (or eating out), and planning fun projects. This subtype can have issues with over-eating, over-talking, and over-stimulation in general.

<u>Type 7 _with Sexual_</u>: The Adventurer. This subtype can be influenced effortlessly and fall into a state of entrainment or fascination by the attraction of new adventures, ideas, and people. Suggestibility, however, works both ways. The sexual Seven also has incredible powers of suggestion and can utilize their charm to lead people into new paradigms, new relationships, new purchases, etc.

<u>Type 7 _with Social_</u>: The Utopian Visionary. The social Seven must balance the need for variety and passion with the need to commit to consistently being a part of a community or group effort. Participation with others imposes personal constraints on how much this subtype can be spontaneous, necessitating personal

sacrifice in order to make arrangements with the group.

* * *

<u>Type 8 *with Self-Preservation*</u>: The Survivalist. In this subtype, the Eight's aggressiveness and abundance are diverted into physical survival and material security. The self-preservation Eight perceives the world as unfriendly, but defends against this passionately. They set out to win or at least go down with a fight and are fiercely defensive of friends and family. This subtype has a tendency to stockpile supplies and mark their territory, which can prove extremely useful in trying times, but can be unnecessarily strenuous during friendlier times.

<u>Type 8 *with Sexual*</u>: The Commander. A sexual Eight utilizes dynamism and self-assertion to get and control the people around them – especially partners or significant others. They are energetic and charismatic, which naturally draws people into their sphere of influence. This subtype consists of born leaders who have power often perceived as strong sexual energy. They go after pleasurable life experiences, including love and sex.

Type 8 _with Social_: The Group Leader. In this subtype, loyalty to friends and social causes outweigh personal needs and feelings. Social Eights direct their intense energy towards a group they can align with and often find themselves in leadership positions. This subtype is the most subdued of the Eights and is often misidentified as Nines or Twos due to an outward focus on helping others. Unlike other Enneatypes, however, social Eights will display control and dominance when engaging with others.

* * *

Type 9 _with Self-preservation_: The Collector. This subtype excels at creating the practical infrastructure and day-to-day habits that support life. However, they often have the tendency to neglect personal health or stuff themselves with food and other sorts of material consumption, and thus are called "Collectors." Efforts toward personal or spiritual growth are often hindered by a life of material abundance and comfort.

Type 9 _with Sexual_: The Seeker. This subtype has a desire to merge either with a partner, spirit, or nature. Sexual Nines often cannot connect with the core of their being, so they replace that with a connection to another person, such as a parent, spouse, or important friend. In day-to-day life, the quest to merge can become problematic as the Sexual Nine does not establish personal boundaries and becomes more and more distant from their own sense of self.

Type 9 _with Social_: The Community Benefactor. This subtype is able to adjust to the style and agenda of their friends and varying social groups. The Social Nine can demonstrate great leadership and selfless contribution for the common good, but also has a tendency to neglect personal priorities to maintain a comfortable social role.

Chapter 14: What now? Practical Uses for the Enneagram

Now that you have discovered the different personality types on the Enneagram, the next step is to apply that knowledge to your day-to-day life. At first glance, it may seem as though this newfound insight into personality is little more than a fun game that lets you compare yourself to other people. However, anyone who makes the mistake of seeing the Enneagram as simply a form of entertainment will lose a valuable opportunity when it comes to making sense of their life and the world around them. Used correctly, the insights offered by the Enneagram can enable you to connect to the core of who you are as a person, recognize and improve on your weaknesses, identify and foster your unique strengths, and develop skills to better understand and relate to the people around you.

It can be a bit of a "lightbulb moment" when you come to realize that not everyone sees the world through the same lens you do. Your first dip into the Enneagram can be both comforting and jarring. On one hand, there is an entire group of people who share your core motivations and fears and with whom you can probably relate more than you ever realized. On the other hand, there is a whole world of other "types" out there, and these people operate, in varying degrees, on what seems like an entirely different value system. Be careful, though, not to confuse "type" with the identity of one's "true self." The Enneagram, rather than being prescriptive and static, is descriptive in nature, covering a dynamic range of integration and stress points. On the surface, what the bare bones of the Enneagram types initially describe is not necessarily your true self but rather the fears and motivations that drive your actions and behaviors. Oftentimes, these fears and motivations set up barriers which actually prevent us from connecting with our true selves. A deeper understanding of those barriers can be the first step in breaking those barriers down and discovering the depth with which you can truly know yourself. Once that breakdown has occurred, you have the choice to offer yourself compassion and forgiveness or to begin the process of rebuilding those same familiar walls between your "personality" and your "true self."

By understanding those things which act as barriers to the discovery of our true selves, we begin to identify our points of weakness and our shortcomings. While this isn't fun for anyone, it's helpful. And not only that; it is essential if one is to achieve true integration and self-knowledge. The Enneagram elucidates the various coping mechanisms we use when under pressure. These are the same coping mechanisms which carried us through our childhood and which we are now experts at employing.

In our adult lives, we become comfortable with coping mechanisms such as "reaction formation" (One) and "overindulgence" (Eight), and we downplay the harmful effects of these defenses by re-labeling them as valued principals like "virtue" and "courage." In true integration, the One finds real virtue, and the Eight demonstrates actual courage, but by leaning too heavily into our coping mechanisms, we risk experiencing only the shadow of what these principals represent.

By shedding light on the root cause of our fears, coping mechanisms, and motivations, we start to understand the patterns which dominate our decision-making processes. Knowing our "blind spots" and the root of these weaknesses has a two-fold effect: It gives us the knowledge necessary to understand and accept our weaknesses, and it gives us the tools necessary to thrive and utilize our strengths so that we might challenge the perceived limitations of our personality.

While we are in the process of integration, or even before we begin any type of journey toward integration, we need to protect ourselves. In life situations where the stakes are high, we can harness the knowledge of our own weaknesses and use that knowledge to help us avoid failure while also maximizing our chance for success.

Of course, living a life of limitation and avoidance isn't quite the key to growth and integration, but we often need to take a step back before we can start climbing, assess our situation, prepare ourselves, and give ourselves the grace of accepting our imperfections before embarking on the upward journey of connection with our true selves. Once we understand the wounds and insecurities that give birth to our weaknesses, we can begin the work of self-forgiveness and self-compassion, and out of that springs the tools we'll use to work towards true self-knowledge.

When a Five begins the process of becoming self-aware, he may seek to take great care when creating a schedule for the week, choosing not to overbook himself with things that do not add value to his life so that he is able to maintain appropriate energy levels and be present for those things which are truly valuable to him. He may also be sure to schedule in time for solitude in an activity which truly refreshes him, whether it be reading, listening to lectures, or engaging in a specialized hobby. By understanding his limits and moving toward a point where he can thrive within them, he may at some point be able to focus his attention outward and maybe even attempt to push those limits ever so slightly.

Instead of denying our weaknesses or trying to "correct" them by counteracting them and pushing our limits, the Enneagram helps us to understand the root cause of our weaknesses and to develop a sense of self-compassion out of which we can thrive and move towards integration.

Albert Einstein once said, "Everyone is a genius. But if you judge a fish by its ability to climb a tree, it will live its whole life believing that it is stupid." Simply put, there are going to be things you're good at, and there are going to be things that make you look like a fish trying to climb a tree. While it's good and healthy to challenge yourself from time to time, you want to avoid the psychological pitfalls that come with perpetually identifying oneself as "the fish that can't climb a tree."

You probably have a pretty good idea of what things you are "good at." Do people gravitate to you when they want advice (Two)? Do they call you up when they want to forget about their problems and do something fun (Seven)? Do they turn to you for pens, information, Band-Aides, etc., knowing that nine times out of ten, you are prepared for everything (Six)?

The Enneagram can help shed light on those things which just come naturally to you, and better, it can help you understand why this is the case. If you are known as a "charmer" (Three), consider your motivations, and then begin to shift that focus from a point where these motivations serve yourself to where your "charm" actually becomes a practice where you genuinely see and acknowledge the good in others. Instead of "flattery," you offer "loving truths." Instead of "performing," you are "connecting."

Each of the nine types has an innate ability to see the world in a unique way. Each of the nine types offers an essential and indispensable gift to the world. A lot of Enneagram literature talks about the weaknesses each type has, and this is not without good reason. What helps us to identify our type tends to be the hang-ups that keep us from being more like the other types, the things that handicap us from having empathy for those who don't think like us. However, by understanding what our weaknesses are, we can move beyond them.

Once you've mastered self-compassion, it's time to move on to empathy, which, when put into action, translates into having compassion for others. One of the most powerful things that the Enneagram does is that it gives us the tools we need to experience the world through others' eyes. While we all have one dominant type, most of us can find at least one or two ways that we can relate to the other types. Who among us has NEVER felt curious or afraid or self-righteous? Just because your dominant type may experience one of these things more intensely than the others doesn't mean you don't, at some level, have something in common with the other eight types. By studying the fears and motivations of each type, we may find that we can identify a little bit with each number. With a little bit of imagination, we can begin to understand what it might be like to experience different aspects of our personality in a more intensified way and to feel overwhelmed by certain thought patterns that our personality may typically repress or avoid.

Once we've gotten in touch with empathy, we can work toward a stance of compassion for others, where we not only understand how others might feel, but we choose to take action by connecting with people on a deeper level. When we understand the various ways that people interpret our behaviors and how our behaviors translate into expressions of value and love, we begin to find creative ways to adjust our stance and the way we communicate. We begin to understand how we can interact with people in a way that communicates value and love as we intend to express it.

By understanding that a Four has a strong need to not only experience each emotion as it comes but also to be understood, you might choose to let him talk through a problem he is having. Instead of offering a quick solution or a distraction, you can challenge yourself to sit in his pain with him, as uncomfortable as that might be, and to connect with him by simply being present.

By understanding that a Nine is likely to deny her own desires for the sake of promoting harmony, you might think to offer choices when deciding on an activity rather than asking "Do you want to [insert what you want to do]?" Along with offering choices, you may also choose to use language which promotes the truth that the Nine in your life matters and that her voice, her desires, and her ideas matter as well.

As we work towards integration, we can hopefully get to a point where value and love, as we understand it, are not defined by the superficialities attached to our specific "type" or how we interpret another's "type" but simply by the understanding that value is innate in us and that love surrounds us. By interacting with others in a way that promotes this truth, we make it possible to establish meaningful relationships.

Our journey of integration begins when we acknowledge our shortcomings and choose to practice self-compassion. As we continue to grow and shift our focus outward, we allow empathy to color our worldview. The path of integration reaches a critical point when we begin to give action to that empathy and manifest compassion for those around us. This outward focus connects us to others, and, ultimately, it is what helps us to realize and connect with our true selves.

Made in the USA
Coppell, TX
16 April 2020

20427548R00113